Living the BIBLE with Children

Living the BIBLE with Children

DOROTHY JEAN FURNISH

with
Carol Johnson
Mary Jo Osterman
Hazel Watts White
Michael E. Williams

Foreword by
Ernest W. Saunders

Abingdon Press
Nashville

LIVING THE BIBLE WITH CHILDREN

Library of Congress Cataloging in Publication Data

FURNISH, DOROTHY JEAN, 1921–
  Living the Bible with children.
  Bibliography: p. 118
  1. Bible—Study. 2. Children—Religious life.
  3. Christian education of children. I. Title.
  BS600.2.F88   268'.432   79-12297

ISBN 0-687-22368-7

MANUFACTURED BY THE PARTHENON PRESS AT
NASHVILLE, TENNESSEE, UNITED STATES OF AMERICA

In memory of
my first religious
education professor,

Alberta Munkres

. . . and my last,

Richard Stanley Ford

Contents

Contributors

CAROL JOHNSON, M.C.E., Garrett-Evangelical Theological Seminary; candidate for M.Div. degree. Extensive experience with liturgical dance; frequent leader of workshops for church school teachers. (" 'Responding out of' the Bible with Dance")

MARY JO OSTERMAN, M.A., Joint Northwestern University–Garrett-Evangelical Theological Seminary Advanced Degree Program; doctoral candidate in Christian Education. Certified laboratory school instructor; lecturer in Christian Education, Garrett-Evangelical Theological Seminary. ("The Total-Environment Way of Teaching")

HAZEL WATTS WHITE, M.C.E., Garrett-Evangelical Theological Seminary; drama studies. Teaches English and creative methodologies in Government Teachers' Training College, Lagos State, Nigeria, West Africa. (" 'Feeling into' the Bible Through Creative Drama")

MICHAEL E. WILLIAMS, M.Div., Garrett-Evangelical Theological Seminary; doctoral candidate in Christian Education in Joint Northwestern University–Garrett-Evangelical Theological Seminary Advanced Degree Program. Extensive experience in theater, creative writing, and storytelling. (" 'Meeting with' the Bible Through Storytelling")

Foreword

To many people, the Bible is an adult book addressed and available to adult readers only. Or so it seems. Its world of camel drivers, fisherfolk, shepherds, and wine merchants is foreign to the world of today's child. Its searchings after religious faith and moral values are too advanced and abstract for the limited comprehension of a child's mind. Its call to faithful existence before God is on a different wavelength than theirs. Others insist that this is God's Word to all, young and old, and they proceed to deal with it as a collection of religious principles and moral values that must be mastered, whether or not they are understood.

Professor Furnish and her associates have a different persuasion. They, too, affirm the central role of the Bible in the education of persons of all ages in the church, but they are concerned primarily with finding ways to do this that are meaningful to and nurturing for children. What does it mean, they ask, to experience the Bible? How can these scenes and sayings affect the life-world of the child in any significant way? They tell us this can happen when these texts are understood to relate the experiences of real persons and are not merely material to be mastered. It can happen when we share understandings with these people of the Bible, participate in their moments of joy and grief, loneliness and acceptance, confusion and conflict, anger and insecurity, and love given and received. As they perceived the presence of the Holy in the midst of daily routines and events, so it becomes possible to perceive that presence in our own moment. This is the word becoming an event; this is the account becoming a happening.

Just as the biblical language is in several forms, so in the varied forms of discourse and prayer, in song and dance, in dramatic enactment and storytelling, in acts of service to community and to individuals, the Bible continues to be heard and responded to today. Nor are these forms of perception and expression to be regarded as optional activities, part of a repertoire of teaching methods to arouse and sustain interest. They are to be seen as meeting places, where the people of the Bible reach out to grasp our hands, confide their story to us, share their anxieties and joys, and lead us to the source of all grace and blessing. Those who make contribution to this book know well enough that no scriptural warning restricts that experience to grownups. Indeed, it is promised to those who are, and to those who are willing to become, little children.

ERNEST W. SAUNDERS
Professor Emeritus of
New Testament Interpretation
Garrett-Evangelical Theological Seminary
Evanston, Illinois

Preface

There are four lifelong Bible-learning tasks that should be begun during the childhood years. The first of these is to experience the content of the Bible so that it becomes a vivid and meaningful part of life. The second is to discover meanings in that content that are related to today's world, and to express those meanings in some appropriate way, either with or without words. The third task is to absorb background information—geography, customs, literary forms—and to learn how the Bible became a book. The fourth task is to acquire simple research skills that make it possible to locate specific passages and to use reference sources, such as Bible dictionaries, commentaries, and atlases. This book focuses on ways to help children accomplish the first two of these four tasks.

The first chapter describes the roots of the dilemma facing those in the present quarter of the twentieth century who wish to teach the Bible to children, and a new way to solve the problem is proposed. In the second chapter, three specific guidelines are offered to facilitate the new proposal. These guidelines provide the theoretical framework for the remainder of the book.

The focus of section 2 is on methodology. Although curriculum resources may suggest dozens of teaching activities, some of these—especially creative drama and dance—are avoided by the average classroom teacher. Still other activities, such as discussion and service projects, are so frequently used that they deserve a new look. And, while they do not avoid storytelling completely, most teachers and parents feel little confidence in their own skills. Each of these teaching methods is discussed in relation to one of the three guidelines.

The chapters in section 2 have been written with the assumption that the reader is an "adventurous amateur." Previous experience with the methods is not necessary, providing the confidence and willingness to risk, characteristic of an adventurer, are present. Parents will find special use for the storytelling skills described in chapter 4 and the conversation skills described in chapter 6.

Section 3 is for those who have been intrigued by the possibilities of this new approach to teaching and want to put it into practice. Chapter 7 gives step-by-step procedures for the use of the three guidelines in planning a session with the Bible as the lesson's primary content. "Advanced amateurs" will be interested in chapter 8, which describes the use of the guidelines in a nonsequential manner in a total-environment way of teaching. Chapter 9 suggests additional learning resources.

The four Bible-learning tasks were first presented in an earlier book, *Exploring the Bible with Children* (Abingdon, 1975). The three guidelines for using the Bible with children are extensions of the point of view first set forth there. The practical implications of the theory were stated in terms of the nature of the settings in which the teaching would take place: group/team teaching, learning centers, and intergenerational models.

In this book, the practical implications are given in terms of specific teaching methods: creative drama, storytelling, dance, discussion, and service projects. Also included here is one setting, a total-environment model for teaching.

While each book can stand alone, each also can supplement the other. There is little duplication of content, but it is intended that the points of view expressed be consistent.

There are many to whom I would like to express gratitude:

- —those who have provided a great stimulus by attending workshops I have led in many states since the publication of *Exploring the Bible with Children*.
- —Carol Johnson, Mary Jo Osterman, Michael E. Williams, and Hazel Watts White, who have contributed chapters in the areas of their specializations.
- —Ernest Saunders, my faculty colleague in New Testament studies, who has graciously accepted the invitation to write the Foreword.
- —the seminary faculty, the president, Merlyn Northfelt, and the dean, Carl Marbury, whose approval of sabbatical made this book possible; and Charlotte Parker and Marilyn Graham, who typed the final manuscript.
- —and finally, my editor, who for the second time has both affirmed and admonished, in her commitment to usability and quality.

D.J.F.

Garrett-Evangelical Theological Seminary

1.
Getting the Book into the Child

This is a book for people who may be uncertain about many aspects of Christian education for children, but who are sure of one thing—the Bible should be an important part of a child's learning. *How* this is to be accomplished can and should be debated, but that it *should* be done is a firm conviction. We want children to know the story of the Christian tradition found in the Bible. Even more compelling, we want children to think of the Bible as their book, not as just a book for their adult future. In order for this to happen, the stories must come alive in such a way that children will feel they have actually participated in the events along with the people of the Bible.

We want children to feel the "holy" as they meet with the biblical text. Just as others through the centuries have found the Bible to be God's Word for them, we want children today to experience the Bible in a way that will open for them new understanding of what it means for persons to encounter God. We want to teach the Bible in such a way that children see beyond the words of the text to the divine at work in the universe.

We want children to find guidance in the Bible for their lives today. This is not an easy goal to accomplish, since there are many differences between the world of the first century and that of the present. Technological achievements and the secularization of society have created problems for today's children that could not have been imagined two thousand years ago. Nevertheless, portions of the Bible, such as the Beatitudes, the Sermon on the Mount, the Ten Commandments, the Great Commandments, the Golden Rule, the Lord's Prayer, and the Twenty-third Psalm provide a time-honored framework of values. In addition to an appreciation of these texts, we can encourage children to continue the search for ultimate values that is recorded in the Bible as a part of our Christian heritage.

Above all, we want children to have a growing, living relationship with the Bible. We know that a ten-year-old child can find more meaning in the story of the prodigal son than most five-year-olds can, and that a teen-ager will probably see greater significance in the story than the ten-year-old. We want, therefore, to introduce each portion of the Bible to children in such a way that its meaning will continue to unfold and deepen throughout their entire lives.[1] This is our primary reason for teaching the Bible to children.

The Problem

So why don't we just do it?

In spite of our certainty that the Bible should be taught, there is an uneasy reluctance to act confidently on our conviction. A brief look at the past and at the way we previously have taught the Bible may help us understand our present dilemma.

Until this century, children were seen as little adults. The Bible was taught as content to be learned, and the teaching process was based on what has come to be known as the transmissive theory. This meant that children were seen as "empty," and the teachers were seen as "full" of knowledge. The task of the teacher was to transmit the knowledge to the children. When a child could say the same words that were in the mind of the teacher, the child was thought to have "learned the lesson."

Teacher   Child

Transmissive Teaching

Fortunately, formal teaching was not the only way children learned the Bible. Its meaning came through home experiences where the Bible was lived, as well as through the culture in which the Bible and Christian symbols were a part of everyday life.

But in the first quarter of the twentieth century, the work of John Dewey and Sigmund Freud began to impress us with the fact that childhood is a distinctive time of life, with values and tasks of its own. This was confirmed by the work of Jean Piaget, and later, Erik Erikson. Although one task of childhood is preparation for adulthood, there came a new recognition of other important tasks for children that made childhood itself more significant. Another new insight was that although children may be able to memorize and recite abstract adult concepts, their intellectual ability often has not yet developed to a point where they are able to understand the concepts. In fact, children may misunder-

17

stand the concepts to such an extent that even in later years they never are able to appreciate them fully.

Once parents and teachers saw for themselves how children learn (which confirmed the work of Piaget and others), a new way of using the Bible with children emerged—to eliminate the teaching of abstractions that have no immediate meaning for children, and instead, to find contemporary content that will relate to their present experiences and needs. In Christian education, we began to affirm that God can be known in ways other than through the Bible. Books written especially for children also can reveal God, so we began to use these to supplement the Bible, and sometimes, instead of the Bible. God can be known through nature, too, so "God's Creation" became a familiar theme. And God is shown through people, so the whole field of human relationships became an important part of Christian education for children.

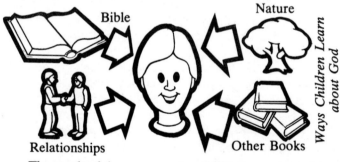

The result of these new understandings was an enriched curriculum, full of biblical values and themes, but the actual Bible content was not as apparent as before. For almost half a century, curriculum planners followed this approach. Eventually, the pendulum began to swing, and an outcry for "more Bible" was heard. In the late 1950s and early 1960s, many denominations revised their curricular offerings with the intention of adding more doctrinal and biblical content. Today new revisions are seeking the same objective. But there is no simple way to go "back to the Bible" as we taught it prior to the turn of this century, because in the meantime we have learned much more about children. Now each time we try to teach the Bible as "knowledge," to children as "minds," we meet that barrier saying, "Children do not understand abstract concepts."

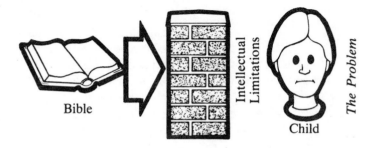

Bible   Intellectual Limitations   Child   *The Problem*

We could ignore the lessons of the past three-quarters of a century and all that it has taught us about children, and go back to the earlier attempt to transfer knowledge from one head to another. Most of us are reluctant to do that. We could give up and say that renewed interest in teaching the Bible to children is a mistake. Few of us are willing to say that. There must be another solution.

One Answer

In recent years we have been helped to see that we are often hampered in the creative solution of problems because we continue to view them from the same old perspective.[2] We sometimes need to hang from the ceiling as we survey a dilemma, rather than always looking at it from the perspective of the floor, with our feet solidly placed.

The traditional perspective has locked us into a kind of circular thinking that leads us nowhere:

1. The Bible is knowledge.
2. Children are minds.
3. Much of the knowledge in the Bible consists of abstract concepts.
4. Children's minds cannot grasp abstract concepts.
5. Therefore, we cannot teach the Bible to children.
6. But we want to teach the Bible to children.
7. Go back to 1.

As long as we begin with the Bible as knowledge and with children as minds, we will always be forced to conclude that teaching the Bible to children is an impossibility.

A new perspective that begins with a different set of assumptions is the only way out. One new way of thinking might look like this:

1. *The Bible is experiences.* It is a record of both the accumulated experiences of the Judeo-Christian communities, and the personal experiences of individuals as they have encountered the Divine in their lives.
2. *Children are experiencers.* They have the ability to understand through their feelings, their curiosities, and their imaginations. They find meaning in the experiences of the here-and-now.
3. *Therefore, we can teach the Bible to children.* With experience as a common denominator between the Bible and children, the barrier of intellectual limitations between the two is torn down, and a clear access is provided.

The Bible as
Experiences

Experience

Feeling

Children as
Experiencers

One Answer

The task, then, is to help children enter into the world of the Bible and experience its content as their own. If we can accomplish this, the meanings of the Bible can be discovered. One way to do this is by experiential teaching.

Teaching Experientially

Teaching the Bible experientially is perhaps more an approach or a mood than a method. It takes into consideration the fact that the Bible records experiences of real people; that the most important aspect of a child's life is the experiences he or she has; that learning means more when it is related to present experiences; and that experiences touch children in all aspects of their lives—their feelings, behavior, intellects, and their ways of making choices.

What is it like to teach the Bible experientially? One way to describe it is to compare it with furniture-making. Some teaching styles are similar to making furniture with a cheap veneer. Just as the veneer is laid on the surface of the wood, the Bible is taught so that its content is only laid on the surface of the child. And just as time and abuse cause the veneer to crack, chip, and eventually peel off, so the learnings are soon forgotten. On the other hand, teaching the Bible experientially resembles making fine furniture of solid wood. As this furniture ages, the beauty deep within continues to show, and may even mellow with the passing of time. When the Bible is taught so that it is an integral part of the child's life, it can be said to have been taught experientially.

Or, compare the result of teaching with a facial expression. We all know that through the magic of greasepaint, circus clowns may wear wide smiles. When the final act has been performed, and the last member of the audience leaves, however, the smile is wiped away. It was only laid on. Teaching the Bible experientially is to teach it in such a way that the smile comes from deep within and cannot be removed as easily as the greasepaint smile.

The very best way to learn is to be an active participant. We think, "How much easier it would be to understand the life and teachings of Jesus if we could have been with him on the hillside as he talked with his followers." Sometimes children, sensing the power of participation, have that same longing to have been a part of New Testament times, as expressed in this song.

> I think when I read that sweet story of old,
> When Jesus was here among men,
> How he called little children as lambs to his fold,
> I should like to have been with them then.
>
> I wish that his hands had been placed on my head,
> That his arm had been thrown around me,
> And that I might have seen his kind look when he said,
> "Let the little ones come unto me."[3]

That desire to experience the Bible is the reason many people travel to the Biblelands. Since none of our children can be transported back in time, and since few of them will be fortunate enough to walk in the footsteps of Abraham and Sarah, Jesus and Mary, or Paul and Priscilla, we must find other ways.

In the next chapter, three guidelines are offered for those who would like to help children experience the Bible content. Section 2 provides directions for specific methods of teaching, based on the three guidelines; and section 3 outlines steps to be followed when preparing lesson plans.

Summary

Many parents and teachers feel frustrated because they find it so difficult to interest children in a study of the Bible. They ask, "How can we get children into the Book?" A well-known religious educator has said that the problem of teaching the Bible to children is not so much getting children into the Book as getting the Book into children.[4]

Whatever teaching methods are finally chosen, the goal always should be to ingrain the Book deep within the child, as beauty is deep within the wood, or as true emotion is deep within the person.

2.
Three Guidelines

It is difficult to imagine the time when the discovery of the common chalkboard was considered a great innovation as an educational method! Perhaps this new method came in response to a generation of teachers who had pleaded, "Give us more ways to make our teaching effective." Today the problem is of a different kind. We often feel overwhelmed by the wide variety of teaching aids available to us. Each day brings announcements of new books containing "proven methods" or audio-visual resources that promise to solve our problems. Many creative teaching methods are at hand, but it is difficult to know which ones to use and the proper time to use them.

A look at some of the basic ingredients in the Bible-teaching process will help us sort out the questions about methodology. First, the children. What are they like? How do they learn? What are their abilities? What are their interests?

Next, there is the Bible. What is its nature? What is its content? What is its significance for Christians today? What results do we hope to achieve by teaching the Bible to children?

Finally, there is the teacher, who asks: How do I help children want to know the Bible? How can I make the Bible more interesting? How can I tell if the children have found meaning in the Bible?

All these questions are related. Questions about children and about the Bible have been answered more fully elsewhere.[1] On the basis of those answers, it is possible to address the "how" questions of the teachers.

As a result of both theoretical formulations and practical experience, three guidelines have emerged for teaching the Bible to children. The first guideline is a way to prepare children to hear the Bible story; the second is a response to the problem of making the Bible interesting; and the third focuses on Bible meanings.

Guideline One

The Bible is a written witness to the experiences of people in the past. It tells of weddings and funerals, feasts and famines. It is about wars between nations and rivalries between brothers and sisters. It portrays hikes on deserts and over mountains, musical instruments, and highway bandits. Through it all there is singing, dancing, praying, and weeping. And it affirms that in such experiences, people saw evidence of God's presence in the world.

Children are people, with an ability to understand things they can see, touch, taste, smell, and feel. Some of their concrete experiences are amazingly parallel to those of people in the Bible. At times children comprehend the events in their lives intellectually, but more often they understand with their emotions and imaginations.

But not all the experiences of modern children are found in the experiences of the Bible. It is a long way from space ships back to camel caravans, or from instantaneous news via satellites and television back to the era of the storyteller who traveled from village to village. A city child finds it difficult to understand the qualities of a man described as being like a good shepherd, and even rural children today rarely watch yeast as it works its miracle in a loaf of bread.

Furthermore, even when the events of the Bible are

similar to those of today, often the interpretations of those events as given by the biblical writers are beyond the understanding of children. They may appreciate the panic of the woman who frantically sought her lost coin, and even may understand why she would want to call in her neighbors for a celebration when it was found, but their world does not help them connect a found coin with "joy before the angels of God over one sinner who repents" (Luke 15:10 RSV).

One bridge between past and present is that people in both worlds share similar emotions. The feelings of joy and sadness, fear and confidence, and anger and love are universal. This is the common ground between the people of the Bible and today's children. Although shepherds and sheep may not be familiar, children can understand needing and receiving care.

The first guideline, then, in helping children experience the Bible, is to enable them to "feel into" the text. When they can feel the same emotions as those felt by the persons in the story, they are well on their way to understanding the story itself. "Feeling into" is similar to preparing the soil for the seed.

Any activity that can help children express emotion is a good "feeling-into" activity. Especially useful are singing, dancing, painting, and creative drama. Less helpful is discussion, unless it is a sharing of feelings about experiences common to the children. The important thing to remember in choosing "feeling-into" activities is that the emotions involved should resemble those in the Bible passage. Here are a few examples.

A Game

If children search until they find a well-hidden coin in the classroom, they will have felt both the frustration of searching for it and the joy of finding it. They can then easily enter into the spirit of the story of the lost coin, because they know how the woman felt.

Painting

If children paint to express how they feel when no one likes them, in the process they will bring to the surface feelings of loneliness, possibly the same as those Zaccheus felt as he sat up in his tree. They will then be ready to "feel" along with Zaccheus, as he marvels at the friendship offered by Jesus.

A Song

If children sing "The Runaway Song"[2] about a child who is assured of a parent's love, they will be able to appreciate the feelings of another runaway, the prodigal son, and his loving father.

Creative Drama

If children have a parade, marching to the strains of an imaginary band and waving imaginary placards, imagining that one of their heroes is present, they will be able to recapture the enthusiasm of the Palm Sunday crowds. They may even be able to feel the disappointment of the masses, when later Jesus turned out not to be the kind of political hero they were looking for.

Or, if through creative drama children can glimpse how it might feel to be captured as slaves, then promised freedom, only to be lost in a desert, and then miraculously saved, they will be able to hear the story of Moses and the Israelites as if it had happened to them.

Creative drama is one of the most effective "feeling-into" activities because it utilizes all the ways people learn: the senses, the body, the imagination, the range of human emotions, and the mental abilities that have been developed. In the process, children experience real feelings.

Guideline Two

One of the tasks of childhood is learning about the adult world and finding appropriate ways to relate to it. The everyday occurrences in which children participate and through which they learn are part of that adult world. They learn acceptable eating habits by observing adults at the table. They learn about the nature of family life by living with a family. They learn to be "street-wise" from their experiences on the street. They learn there is a world beyond the home as they see their parents leave for work, as the family participates in community activities, and as they see older brothers and sisters leave for school. Because all these are observable and present experiences, it is comparatively easy for children to relate to them.

For those of us in the Christian community, the Bible is an important part of our adult world. But because it records past events in which children did not participate, it is more difficult for them to understand it. However, even though it is difficult, the sharing of this tradition, by one generation with the next, is one of the ways religious development takes place.

Most children cannot comprehend the biblical text in even the most contemporary versions. Those who try are often discouraged and write off the Bible forever as an extremely dull, confusing book that has no meaning for them. The Bible needs a teacher, someone who can convey the traditional words so that they move with vitality out of the past into the child's present world. It needs a teacher who can make the events of the past so real that the Bible becomes an Event in the child's life.

The second guideline is to help children "meet with" the text in an exciting and involving way. The "meeting with" is the planting of the seed into the soil that has been prepared with "feeling-into" activities. If the "feeling-into" step has been a dynamic experience, the "meeting-with" stage is simple. However, if it has been difficult to capture the emotions of the Bible passage in the first step, then "meeting with" must carry a larger share of the burden.

To "meet with" the Bible is much like receiving a snapshot on which is pictured a small segment of human experience. Some children may never have heard the story of the triumphal entry into Jerusalem, for example. You, as the teacher, have helped them "feel into" the story by having a parade for a present-day hero. The "meeting with" begins when you say, "When Jesus and his disciples came closer to Jerusalem, he said to them. . . ," and the "meeting with" ends as soon as the biblical narrative has concluded. When you began, the children had never heard the story, and when you are finished, they have heard it. They have "met with" the biblical text. For children who have heard the story before, the "meeting with" will be like seeing a shapshot of a familiar scene, but one that has been taken from a different point of view. In this step there is no introduction or discussion of the text—only the giving and receiving of the "snapshot."

The most appropriate methods for "meeting with" are those that are most likely to stimulate the child to say, "It feels as if I am really there!" Commercial sources have appreciated the difficulty of this part of the process and have flooded the market with cassette tapes, filmstrips, records, motion pictures, flannelgraphs, puppets, and similar items. Many of these are excellent, especially when used along with "feeling-into" and "responding-out-of" activities. Usually, however, they cannot stand alone and they never can substitute for a well-prepared teacher.

Here are some ways adults can help children "meet with" the content of the Bible.

Slides or Filmstrips

Slides and filmstrips are static media, so when these are used to tell a story, more attention must be given to the "feeling-into" activities. The addition of a sound track increases their value in capturing the interest and imagination of children.

Motion Pictures

Dramatic, well-produced motion pictures, which take into account the abilities of children to understand, can be almost as effective in making the Bible live, as if the children had been part of the actual event. The disadvantages of this form include cost, availability, and the difficulty of finding films that do not stress a particular interpretation.

Cassette Tapes and Records

Tapes and records that give a dramatic presentation of a Bible story can be more effective than filmstrips or slides, since they encourage the child's own imagination to create the pictures.

Songs

Music that tells the Bible story is inexpensive, and especially effective, because the song can be repeated many times without loss of interest. In fact, the more familiar a song becomes, the more it will be requested by the children. Melodies once learned return to mind again and again, and each time, will remind the child of the words.

Reading Aloud

When it is anticipated that reading aloud from the Bible will provide the major "meeting-with" experience, the reading must be extremely well done and accompanied by intense "feeling-into" and "responding-out-of" activities. Reading may be used most effectively in connection with other "meeting-with" activities. For example, after the children have learned and enjoyed the song, "A Certain Traveler,"[3] the story of the good Samaritan then could be read from the Bible.

Storytelling

Storytelling is perhaps the best method for helping children "meet with" the Bible. It costs nothing, it is always available, and it helps children experience the way the Bible was handed down to us through oral tradition. Most of all, storytelling becomes a living symbol of the desire of one generation to pass on its tradition to the next. And when the story is finished, the storyteller is still there for the next phase of the Bible-teaching process.

Guideline Three

Children respond in some way to every experience in their lives. Sometimes they respond with words. Often they jump, run, clap, sing, or cry. At other times they may withdraw and seem not to respond at all, but even withdrawal is a definite response. Without some observable response, a teacher does not know what has been learned and consequently is not able to make plans for the next sequence of learning activities.

The writers of the Bible have recorded for us responses to experiences of divine presence. Moses' experience—God in a burning bush—was not the climax of that event, but only the beginning. God called for an action response from Moses when he declared, "I will send you to Pharaoh that you may bring forth my people, the sons of Israel, out of Egypt" (Exodus 3:10). Isaiah's vision of God concluded with a commitment response, "Here am I! Send me" (Isaiah 6:8*b*). After affirming the worth of persons by saying that we are like the salt of the earth and the light of the world, Jesus called on his hearers to respond with a quality of life: "Let your light so shine before men, that they may see your good works and give glory to your Father who is in heaven" (Matthew 5:16). When the rich man sought the way to eternal life, Jesus suggested that he sell what he had and give the money to the poor. He, too, responded: He went away sorrowful (Matthew 19:22).

The Bible as God's word is not only to be heard but requires a response from us.

The third guideline, then, in helping children experience the Bible is to encourage them to "respond out of" their encounter with the Bible text. This guideline is both biblically and theologically sound. If the Bible has been experienced through "feeling into" and an experiential "meeting with," a response of some kind will be inevitable. This response may be likened to the harvest that follows the planting of the seed in the prepared soil.

Three Guidelines

The teacher's task is to provide the classroom climate for a positive response. This may mean simply hearing and accepting the spontaneous comments or unspoken responses that come at the close of the story or other activity. It may mean making plans that will draw out or help children express what they feel but have not said. It will also suggest that you, as teacher or parent, share what the text means to you, since this exchange is an important part of teaching.

When children are asked to express their feelings and ideas, care should be taken that their comments not be formulated so as to please the teacher. The suspicion that this often may happen has given rise to the unfortunate phrase "Sunday school answers." These kinds of answers are of no help to either the teacher or the child.

Not all responses will be directly related to the Bible itself. Some may be connected only vaguely: "That reminds me of once when we were in Colorado. . . ." Others may show reactions to the activity itself: "The man on the record who read the story had a funny voice!" Still another response may relate to the physical setting or to something that happened before the child left home. These do not fit naturally into the teacher's lesson plan, but they are valid responses for the children who make them, and need to be heard and acknowledged, even if only nonverbally.

There are four types of relevant responses that might follow "meeting with" a Bible passage: feeling, thinking, acting, and deciding.

Feeling Responses

After "meeting with" Psalm 100, children might feel like jumping for joy. Feelings about a "meeting with" the Lord's Prayer might be summarized through creative dance. After "meeting with" Zaccheus, children might be ready to sing their feelings.

> I like me just the way I am,
> You like me just the way I am,
> God likes me just the way I am,
> Sing Glory Hallelujah.[4]

Thinking Responses

Questions and answers and discussion are traditional ways in which we have led children to respond to Bible passages. Most prepared curriculum resources contain many examples of this kind of material.

Other possible thinking responses include creative writing of all kinds: litanies, plays, stories, newspaper accounts, scripts for slides or pictures, paraphrases of Bible selections, and words for songs. (Teachers sometimes assume that writing a Bible story in the form of a play, for example, is a "meeting-with" activity, but this is not so. To write a play, the children would have had to "meet with" the Bible story previously in some other way.)

Thinking need not always be an end in itself. When children are reluctant to express their feelings without words, a conversation might remind them of the feelings they had, and the session then might climax with a wordless feeling-response activity.

Acting and Deciding

Perhaps the most difficult form of response to the Bible is constructive action of some kind. For children, as well as for adults, it is usually easier to respond with words or with feelings. An extensive discussion of this aspect of "responding out of" will be found in chapter 6, " 'Responding out of' the Bible in Word and Deed."

Summary

Bible teaching need not be a bore. But if it is to be a dynamic, life-renewing experience for children, it must treat the child as a whole person. The first step is to prepare the soil by helping the children feel the emotions inherent in the Bible story or passage to be taught. The second step is to plant the seed—to present the text as accurately and as effectively as possible, so the children will feel that they themselves were participants in the event. The third step is to reap the harvest by encouraging and accepting the children's responses to the Bible text.

3.
"Feeling into" the Bible
Through Creative Drama*

"Ask the children to dramatize the story." When a Bible story is part of the lesson plan, this is almost always one of the suggestions in the teacher's guidebook. But very often teachers replace dramatization with a more familiar method—one that requires less risk. This chapter attempts to take some of the mystery—and therefore some of the risk—out of the general approach to teaching known as creative dramatics.

The emphasis is on the way creative drama can prepare children to hear the Bible story, but it also describes how, after hearing the story, children can respond through dramatization.

Creative Drama's Watchword: Process, Not Product

A polished production for a critical audience is not the purpose of creative drama. Creative drama emphasizes the process rather than the product, and the process is for the sake of the child. In an informal classroom setting, and through the use of dramatic techniques, children are guided in learning activities that transport them out of the here-and-now into a world of imagination. It is this ability to

*Written by Hazel Watts White.

transcend time and space that makes creative drama uniquely effective in helping children experience the content of the Bible. Through creative drama, a child for a time can be Noah adrift in the ark, David in battle with Goliath, Mary or Martha in conversation with Jesus, or Paul bound in prison chains.

Five Keys to Creative Drama

Those who use creative drama will need to understand and act in relation to five key words: trust, freedom, imagination, concentration, and motivation. Although they are not in "five easy lessons," when you understand these concepts you will be ready to experiment with creative drama in your church school class.

Trust

It is important that each child trust you as a leader. Children will depend on you for direction and guidance. Establish that trust in the beginning by working with them, so that they know what is expected. In an approach that requires freedom, rules may seem to be undesirable constraints. On the contrary, simple ground rules established by you and the group together actually free children to create and also provide the trust in you that is needed to assure them of a secure setting.

Freedom

Freedom to move about the room is necessary. Creative drama requires no props or furniture, but it does require open space. If your classroom is small, before the children come, move the chairs against the wall and create open space in the center of the room. The children should be able to move freely around the whole area without crowding or bumping into each other.

Freedom also means permission to move freely. This is a sharp contrast to the traditional Sunday school rule, "Be quiet and sit still!" The children will sense this permission through your acceptance of their spontaneity and because the climate of trust has been built.

Imagination

Imagination is your special tool. Inside each of us is that very special gift of creativity that is waiting to be shared. Many times we make the mistake of asking children to "pretend." Using imagination is vastly different from pretending, for pretending is make-believe, but imagination is a very real experience. With our imaginations we can go anywhere in the world. We can look into the past or move into the future. We can be adults, children, or animals at any given time. Imagination is absolutely necessary, because without it, there could be no creative drama.

Concentration

It is important that children learn to concentrate. Imagination has no limit. Children have exciting and unusual thoughts. They must hold those creative thoughts long enough to develop them into some kind of action. Simple warm-up activities are intended to help children put aside the mundane and, through concentration, discover and use their powers of imagination. For example, they might be asked to imagine that they are listening to a big pot of chocolate boiling. Images and odors will immediately come to their minds, but unless captured, they will fade quickly away. If some specific questions are asked, those immediate responses can be sustained, made conscious, and then expressed through creative drama.

What does it smell like?
What does it look like?
Imagine what happens when the chocolate in this giant
    pot is poured into large cooling pans.
Can you taste it?

All these questions require concentration. But what a delightfully rewarding experience! The more you work with your group, the less time you will need to spend on warm-ups such as this. They are always necessary, however, because children come into the classroom from different situations. They need help in moving from a real world into an imaginary one. So turn them on! Watch the wheels go round, the doors unlock, and the lights gleam in their eyes when they discover that you appreciate their creative minds and those hidden thoughts and ideas that they now feel free to express. They have kept all those wonderful things to themselves and now, unlike many adults, you, their teacher, have provided a place where those ideas are allowed expression.

Motivation

Motivation is the way you move from simple concentration warm-ups into activities that point directly to the Bible passage you want the children to experience. The motivation activity is the part of the session that plows up and prepares the soil, so that when the seed is planted—the story told—it is almost impossible for it not to take root.

The five key words just described, viewed together, constitute a minicourse in the theory of creative drama. The next two parts of this chapter deal with how-to questions.

You will discover how to plan for a session, with the story of Moses and the Exodus as the Bible content. Then you will be able to visualize the classroom situation you have planned, as you read about an actual session using that story.

Preparing to Use Creative Drama

There are four steps to follow as you prepare to teach a Bible story through the use of creative drama: (1) choose a story; (2) identify feelings; (3) plan a motivational activity; and (4) plan some warm-up activities.

Choose a Story

Many stories in the Bible reveal the emotional experiences of the people of those times. Children can understand and appreciate the beautiful and rich heritage of Christianity when they have the opportunity through their imaginations to share sympathetically in the experiences of Bible people. So choose a story. When you select a story for dramatization, always look for one in which the characters engage in some kind of physical action, and where there are emotions associated with that action that can be understood by children. (For more criteria on story choice, see chapter 4.)

Let's suppose you have chosen the story of Moses and the Exodus. With the help of the Bible, Bible commentaries, or your teacher's guidebook, you will want to review the details and flow of the story.

> The children of Israel were captured and enslaved by the Egyptians. They were treated very cruelly. They were forced to make bricks with straw. In fact, Pharaoh said to the slave driver, "You must no longer give these people straw for making bricks. After this, let them go and gather straw for themselves. But you must demand

from them the same number bricks they have been making. Don't listen to their crying, for they are lazy; that is why they are crying."

The sun was very hot and there was little food or water. The children of Israel prayed to God for freedom. God heard their cries and sent Moses to free them from their captors and to lead them to a land that had been promised to them. God spoke to Moses and sent him to tell Pharaoh, "Let my people go." Moses obeyed God's command. His task was not easy, for the Pharaoh was cruel and stubborn.

But finally Moses led the children of Israel out of captivity through the desert to a beautiful place they called the land of milk and honey.

This is the story you want the children to experience for themselves, so that they will feel that they are really the enslaved children of Israel. How will you begin?

Identify Feelings

Reread the story of Moses and identify the emotions you would like your children to feel when they hear it. As prisoners and slaves, the people must have felt sadness, fear, and weariness; but because they trusted Moses to lead them to the promised land, they were finally able to feel hope, joy, and gratitude. And how must Moses have felt, having been chosen by God for such a responsibility? Perhaps he was both proud to have been chosen and afraid he might fail. All these emotions are familiar to children because they have experienced them in their own lives.

Plan a Motivational Activity

Plan a motivational activity that stimulates the children to create or recall the feelings you found in the story. This is the "feeling-into" activity that motivates them to listen intently when the story is told. The motivational activity will be a contemporary experience, something that could happen in the children's world today. It should contain the same feelings as in the Bible story, but it should not use any of the events in that story.

> The whole class is aboard an airplane. They are very excited because, for the first time, they are leaving America to visit another country. Suddenly the plane is forced to land. Their excitement turns to anxiety and fear. They land in the burning hot desert. There is no water in sight. Eventually they are rescued, but not until they have had some very difficult experiences.

When children play this scene, there will be opportunities for expressions of joy, excitement, fear, anxiety, hope, and gratitude. And when these feelings have surfaced, the children will be ready to hear the story of Moses.

Plan Warm-Up Exercises

Finally, think through some warm-up exercises in which you can lead the children before you begin the motivational activity just outlined. These need not be formal, but they will prepare the children for a session during which they will be asked to use both imagination and concentration. Here are some suggestions.

1. Physical activities. Engage children in rhythms that require them to move around the room. Ask them to imagine they are looking for a lost ring, or that they are at the airport watching a plane come in.

2. Sensory awareness exercises. Choose several objects that make different sounds. Place them on a table. Ask for two or more volunteers to look at the objects and then to

listen while you make a sound with each and call it by name. Then ask them to sit down with their backs to the table, close their eyes and listen to all the sounds again, naming each as it is made. Some objects that work well are rocks, keys, empty glasses, erasers, and blocks of wood. This is a challenge. Give each person two turns to get the right answer. The number of sounds may be increased to as many as will hold the attention of the children. Always begin with three, increasing to more.

Try some other sensory awareness exercises. Ask children to smell something pleasant, such as cookies baking, or perfume; then ask them to smell something unpleasant. Suggest that they taste a piece of candy; then suggest that they taste something bitter.

It is best if the warm-ups can lead directly into the motivational activity. In the following session, a warm-up activity prepares the children for the forced landing of the plane in the desert, and creative drama techniques are illustrated.

A One-Hour Session Using the Story of Moses

The key words basic to creative drama and the preparation plans just previewed are now woven together to create a lesson plan. It includes elements of the captivity, the years of wandering in the desert as the children of Israel sought freedom, and the eventual rescue.

√ Create a Classroom Climate

1. Establish trust. Before you begin your creative drama session, talk with the children about the rules of play. You are their leader. Let the children know that you are there to guide them and that together you will have an enjoyable

Living the Bible with Children

time. They need only to listen to the sound of your voice at all
times because your voice will tell them what to do. (Since the
leader must never lose control of the group, two words are
very important: "Action" and "Cut." They work with all age
levels. Action means to move, and Cut means to stop
immediately.)

2. Allow free movement. Give children their space.
Show them the area they will be free to use, and let them
explore that area fully; the floor, the walls and ceiling, and all
the space in-between.

*"Let me see if you can walk on every spot in this drama
area. Cover every inch and corner of it—the sides, the middle,
all of it."*

The children will move all around the room, and in this
way they will discover that they need not restrict themselves
to little groups in the center.

√ *Provide a Warm-Up Exercise to Encourage Imagination
and Concentration*

Now ask the children to stand up and to imagine that this
space is a very hot desert.

*"You are walking through the hot sand. Without talking to
anyone, show me with your bodies what is happening in this
desert."*

Watch the responses for a few minutes.

*"Now stop and rest a while. I can see that you are very,
very hot and thirsty."*

Allow some seconds for them to express their need for
water and cool shade.

*"Look! What is that on the ground in front of you? There's
a rope sticking up out of the sand. Maybe it will uncover a well*

of water. Reach down and pull it. Pull harder! STAND UP and pull! YOU'RE NOT PULLING HARD ENOUGH! PULL . . . PULL . . . Cut."

Through this exercise, you have stimulated the children's imaginations as to what it is like to be lost and to wander in the desert. Through your words and the tone of your voice you have helped them hold their thoughts long enough to be able to express them in action. It takes concentration to recall how it feels to be hot, tired, and thirsty. It also requires both imagination and concentration to pull strenuously on a rope. The children are now ready for the next step.

√ *"Feeling into": Use a Motivational Activity*

Direct the children to sit down in a semicircle.

"Please listen to my voice, because we are getting ready to travel to another country. Let's imagine that all of us are going aboard an airplane. We are beginning a trip to a very exciting but unknown country. Now get into the airplane; show me how you feel and what you are doing."

Children will move into position in the space cleared for activity. Listen to them and watch them. Join them and say very seriously,

"May I have your attention, please? Do not panic! We are having engine trouble and will be forced to land in the desert below. Please fasten your seat belts. Remember, do not panic! . . . As quickly and as carefully as possible, get out of this plane, and find a place to camp until the engine has been repaired, or until help comes. Let's go! . . . My goodness, it's like a furnace out here. I can hardly breathe. We must find some water soon. (Continue walking and searching for water.) *Do you see any trees? If you can see trees, there will be*

water nearby . . . Stop! What is that? I hear noises. It's a helicopter!!! (Children will respond.) *Help has come! Now we will have water!"*

Allow the children to respond for a few seconds and then say "Cut!" Gather once again in the semicircle.

"Let's talk about what happened to us. How did you feel?"

Allow a few minutes for children to talk about the experience. Children may reply with comments such as: "I was excited and happy at first, but later I was scared." "I really felt hot and thirsty. My throat was so dry."

"How did you feel when you saw the helicopter?"

Some may respond with: "Yeah!" "Happy!" "I jumped up and down and started to wave to it!"

√ *"Meeting with": Tell the Story of Moses and the Exodus*

The motivational activity just described has helped the children feel the same emotions that the children of Israel must have felt as they wandered in the desert seeking the promised land. Through this experience, the children have "felt their way into" the Bible story. They are now ready to hear the story itself. Ask the children to return to the semicircle.

"Do you know that some people many years ago had an experience similar to yours?"

Follow this with a simple telling of the Bible story. Use your own resumé of the story in Exodus or the story as told in a book of Bible stories.

√ *"Responding out of": Dramatize the Story*

Some children have responded to this approach spontaneously by asking to dramatize the Moses story. Here is one way to help them do that.

After you have finished telling the story, ask the children to identify the key characters in the story and to decide among themselves which roles they will play. Do not assign roles; let the children select their own characters—they will respect them more. Remember, it is the process and not the product that is important. If children choose a girl to play the part of Moses, that is perfectly all right.

Next, decide on a scenario:

> You are enslaved by Pharaoh's soldiers. They are forcing you to make bricks without straw. Moses will come and free you and you will move to another place. All parts of the drama will be played in this room. We will make the transfer of time and space in our imaginations.

If there is not enough time to do both the motivational activity and the story dramatization, the dramatization can be saved for the next session. At that time give a brief review of what happened the week before, to remind them how they were feeling at the end of the session; then move directly into the dramatization of the story.

After the story has been dramatized, take a few minutes to talk about the positive aspects of the experience, and let them share how they could improve their play if they did it again. If time permits, a replay will further reinforce the impact of the story.

It is important to emphasize that the response to the story need not be in drama, just because creative drama was used to lead into the storytelling. You or the children might have chosen dance, discussion, painting, or some other method for the response.

Living the Bible with Children

Summary

Creative dramatics is a process that helps children "feel into" the Bible as they identify with biblical characters and share their emotions. It also provides a way for children to respond to their experience of the Bible content. Trust, freedom to move, concentration, and motivation all are important. But the most valuable tool is the imagination of the child. Through this process the child not only hears the Bible story, but lives it as well. The Bible will be much more meaningful both to you and to the children because you have dared to be creative!

4.
"Meeting with" the Bible Through Storytelling*

Storytelling is one of the most ancient customs of the human race. For untold centuries people have gathered as families and in larger groups to share their experiences, dreams, and fantasies in stories. Some of those tales belonged to the entire community and were told again and again. Creation stories gave the people knowledge of their origins and explained how their world came into being. Legends and histories told them where their ancestors had traveled. Other stories pointed out those qualities that were of value and attempted to interpret the deepest mysteries of the world. As children in communities listened to story-tellers, they began to know and experience the traditions of their people.

The Bible is a reservoir of such stories and images that all Christians share, and many are shared with members of the Jewish community, as well, through the Old Testament. Many were passed down from generation to generation long before they were ever recorded in written form. Even though our interpretations of these stories may differ, we are united by this common heritage.

The Value of Storytelling

Through storytelling, four areas of human experience are enriched for both the tellers and the hearers:

*Written by Michael E. Williams.

(1) imagination; (2) relationships; (3) feelings; and
(4) response.

Imagination

Imagination is a human being's ability to experience
events, persons, and things that are not physically present.
We experience the events that take place in our imagination
with all our senses. It is the place of memories, dreams, and
fantasies. Sometimes people have viewed the imagination
with disfavor, saying, "That's just your imagination."
Recently psychologists and philosophers have begun to
discover the truth that poets, artists, and storytellers have
known for centuries—what we remember of the past and
what we hope for in the future depend upon our ability to
participate in the sights and sounds of our imaginations.

Pictures, books, slides, films, and television provide
ready-made images, but storytelling encourages both those
who tell and those who listen to exercise their imaginations
by creating their own images. Through imagination, children
are able to transport themselves to other places and other
times, and in this way they can begin to enter into the
experiences of persons who lived long ago in Bible times.

Relationships

There are three primary relationships involved in any
storytelling experience. First, we come to know the story in
the person of the storyteller. Through the teller's words, the
story world is created and presented to those gathered to
listen. In that moment the story exists in the relationship
between the teller and the hearers.

Second, as the story is told, we come to know and care
about the persons who inhabit that story world. The

characters of the story then become a part of our experience that is carried into our daily lives.

Third, storytelling is a public act. A story does not live until it is shared. Those who have experienced the story together become a community created by the story world they have shared. Therefore, as tellers and as hearers, we can find a relationship to the church community by the stories we have told and heard there.

Storytelling is an especially appropriate way to help children "meet with" the Bible because it is an experience through which children can come to know and care about the teller, the persons in the story, and the community that shares the story.

Feelings

As we listen to stories, the characters and events of each story come to us not as themes or meanings but as persons and events. Stories may excite, anger, soothe, or confuse us, but when they are told well, we are touched by the world they create. Some stories can transform our lives and radically change the way we view the world. Many of the parables told by Jesus often overturn what we have been taught to expect. It must have startled his listeners when Jesus told a story in which an outcast Samaritan showed greater compassion than did the accepted religious leaders.

Response

Finally, stories provide an experience to which persons can respond. The response may take the form of another story, a dance, a painting, or a poem. Each time a story is told, it becomes a new event. Each time the story is heard, we discover a new delight and depth, which in turn open unexplored possibilities for response out of the experience.

Preparing to Tell a Story

Few of us feel confident as storytellers, especially as tellers of Bible stories. When the church school teacher's guidebook suggests that we tell a story from Scripture, most of us resort to reading the text directly from the Bible or from a Bible storybook. This is not necessary, because storytelling is not that difficult. Here some ways to prepare and present Bible stories are suggested. These methods require no special training beyond an interest in becoming a better storyteller and a willingness to invest the time and effort required to prepare the story well.

The process involves three stages: (1) choosing the story; (2) getting to know the story; and (3) practicing the story.

Choosing the Story

Church school instructional materials usually suggest the Bible selection most appropriate for the session. In these cases, the choice has been made for you, and you can proceed to prepare the story for telling. If, however, you find yourself in charge of a class, an informal gathering of children, or an intergenerational event for which there is no prescribed lesson plan, or if you are a parent who wishes to tell stories at home, you must first choose a story. Often the first choice is a story that is a favorite of yours. Though this is a natural tendency, this method of choice severely limits the possibilities.

The four areas of human experience enriched by storytelling can serve as guides. Begin by asking yourself (the teller) questions about the story, relating these areas. Does the story spark my *imagination?* Are the characters in the story significant enough to make a *relationship* with them important? Does the *feeling* of the story move me deeply, make me laugh, cry, think? Is it rich enough in characters and action that I could hear it again and again, *responding* to different aspects of the story each time? The more often you are able to answer yes to these questions, the better you will be able to tell the story so that it will have meaning for your listeners.

The next step is to ask certain questions about the relationship of the story to those who will hear it. Will the story exercise the *imaginations* of children, even if its images are understood concretely? Are the characters of the story valuable additions to the community of persons and characters with whom the child is already in *relationship*? Does the story have *feelings* within it with which the children can identify? Will the story encourage a variety of creative *responses*? Yes answers to these questions indicate that the story has a potential for providing a meaningful experience for both the teller and the listeners.

Getting to Know the Story

Storytellers need to be freed from the idea that a story must be memorized. In fact, memorization can stand in the way of good telling. A memorized story is always in someone else's words, rather than your own. A story that is memorized is not flexible enough to allow for elaboration or simplification as the situation demands; if children interrupt in the middle of a story with a question or comment on the action, memorization does not allow you to respond without shattering the world created by the story.

If you are not going to memorize a story, you will need another way to recall it so that you can tell it with confidence. Some very short stories may be remembered simply by going over the events until their order is learned. There is another method useful for learning longer, more complex stories.

This technique is called scoring, and is an adaptation of a design by Barbara McDermitt of the School of Speech at Northwestern University.[1]

A score for a story is much like the score for a piece of music. In a story score, instead of notes, there are word clues for the teller. Both scores are divided into units of action; in music, these units are called measures, but in a story score, they are called scenes. When the setting changes, or when a new character appears, the story moves to a new scene. Finally, both musical and story scores always use the same general format. Rather than being a musical "staff," the story format is a grid that looks like this.

	PLACE	CHARACTERS	OBJECTS	ACTIONS
Scene 1.				
Scene 2.				
Scene 3.				

The story of the feeding of the five thousand can be used to show how a story score is created. Since there are four versions of this event in the Gospels, you are faced with the necessity of choosing a source for your story (Matthew 14:13-21; Mark 6:30-44; Luke 9:10-17; John 6:1-15). You can choose the story as told in one of the Gospels, including only the details found there, or you can combine the elements from two or more of the Gospels to create your own version of the story. The most familiar example of this approach is the way we tell the Christmas story, taking the wise men and the flight into Egypt from Matthew, and from Luke, the shepherds in the fields. Yet another source from which to choose the story version would be a book of Bible stories.[2] Regardless of the source chosen, you, as teller, are free to use your knowledge of Bible backgrounds to expand on the description of characters and events so that the listeners may experience the world of the story more fully.

Now you are ready to work through the story scene by scene. For the purpose of this illustration, materials were drawn from all four Gospel accounts.

In scene 1, Jesus hears of the death of John and tells the disciples he wants to get away from the crowd and be alone.

	PLACE	CHARACTERS	OBJECTS	ACTIONS
Scene 1.	crowded city	Jesus & disciples John crowd		hears of John's death; goes to be alone

Scene 2—the boat trip of Jesus and the disciples on the Sea of Galilee to a place near Bethsaida. Here the change of location signals a different scene.

	PLACE	CHARACTERS	OBJECTS	ACTIONS
Scene 2.	Sea of Galilee	Jesus & disciples	boat	sails to Bethsaida

Scene 3 takes us back to the crowd Jesus left, who, hearing where he is going, follow along a land route by foot, by donkey, cart, and wagon, in order to arrive at Bethsaida ahead of him. A change of both character and location indicates a change of scene here.

	PLACE	CHARACTERS	OBJECTS	ACTIONS
Scene 3.	crowded city	crowd	feet donkeys carts wagons	crowd follows Jesus

In scene 4, Jesus and his disciples bring the boat to shore near Bethsaida, only to find the crowd already waiting.

	PLACE	CHARACTERS	OBJECTS	ACTIONS
Scene 4.	country-side near Bethsaida	Jesus & disciples crowd	boat shore	Jesus lands, crowd is waiting

In scene 5, Jesus has compassion on the crowds of people and begins to teach and heal them in spite of his own grief.

	PLACE	CHARACTERS	OBJECTS	ACTIONS
Scene 5.	country-side near Bethsaida	Jesus crowd		Jesus has compas-sion; teaches and heals

Scene 6 begins on the evening of the same day. Note that a time change signals a scene change here. The disciples suggest that Jesus send the crowd to the city to find food.

	PLACE	CHARACTERS	OBJECTS	ACTIONS
Scene 6.	country-side near Bethsaida	Jesus & disciples crowd	food	disciples want to send crowd away

In scene 7, Jesus tells the disciples to feed the crowd from the food they brought with them. The disciples reply that they have only five loaves of bread and two fish. John's Gospel says this food is offered by a child.

	PLACE	CHARACTERS	OBJECTS	ACTIONS
Scene 7.	country-side near Bethsaida —evening	Jesus & disciples crowd	5 loaves 2 fish	Jesus tells disciples to feed crowd

In scene 8, the crowd is seated in smaller groups. Jesus blesses the loaves and the fish and tells his disciples to pass the food among the crowd.

	PLACE	CHARACTERS	OBJECTS	ACTIONS
Scene 8.	country-side near Bethsaida —evening	Jesus & disciples crowd	5 loaves 2 fish	crowd sits in groups; Jesus blesses food; disciples distribute food

During scene 9, the crowd eats its fill and there are twelve basketsful left over. And the story says there were over five thousand people gathered there.

	PLACE	CHARACTERS	OBJECTS	ACTIONS
Scene 9.	country-side near Bethsaida —evening	over 5,000 people	12 bas-ketsful leftover pieces	crowd eats fill

Having completed the scoring process, the finished score would look like this:

	PLACE	CHARACTERS	OBJECTS	ACTIONS
Scene 1.	crowded city	Jesus & disciples John crowd		hears of John's death; goes to be alone
Scene 2.	Sea of Galilee	Jesus & disciples	boat	sails to Bethsaida
Scene 3.	crowded city	crowd	feet donkeys carts wagons	crowd follows Jesus
Scene 4.	countryside near Bethsaida	Jesus & disciples crowd	boat shore	Jesus lands, crowd is waiting
Scene 5.	"	Jesus crowd		Jesus has compassion; teaches and heals
Scene 6.	" —evening	Jesus & disciples crowd	food	disciples want to send crowd away
Scene 7.	"	"	5 loaves 2 fish	Jesus tells disciples to feed crowd

"Meeting with" the Bible Through Storytelling

Scene 8.	country-side near Bethsaida —evening	Jesus & disciples crowd	5 loaves 2 fish	crowd sits in groups; Jesus blesses food; disciples distribute food
Scene 9.	"	over 5,000 people	12 basketsful leftover pieces	crowd eats fill

After you have created and used a score, you will want to keep it to refresh your memory when you have occasion to tell the story again at some future time.

Practicing the Story

A certain amount of practice may be done alone. But before the story is told in public, it should be practiced aloud several times for one or more persons, preferably near the age of your anticipated audience. Tell the story as often as you can, for the more often you tell it, the sooner it will become your own.

The score provides only the skeleton of the story. As it is practiced you will elaborate by adding details to create the sights, sounds, odors, and other sensory experiences of the world in which the story takes place. In the feeding of the five thousand, the soft rhythmic splashing of the sea, the creaking of the boat, and the aroma of the bread and fish can excite the imagination. However, it is important that the addition of detail does not stop the flow of the story's action. This is especially crucial with young children, because it is the action that holds their attention.

Practicing a story involves a great deal more than learning and rehearsing the basic plot. It is the time when the world of the story is created in detail. Through practice, the story becomes your story as you learn to tell it in your own words. And finally, practice allows you to develop enough flexibility so that you can adapt the story readily to various audiences and situations.

Telling the Story

At last comes the day you have been preparing for. It is time to tell the story. You will need to be aware of several things.

The Room

Are the listeners facing away from a door or window that might otherwise prove distracting? Are you sitting where you can be seen by all? Are the listeners sitting so that you can maintain eye contact, even with those on the outer edge of the group?

The Age of Your Audience

Different aspects of a story will appeal to different age groups. While action may hold the attention of younger children, the characters in the story may attract older ones. Even if the story is suitable for the age of your listeners, you will hold their interest more closely by directing it to their level of experience.

The Attention of Your Listeners

It is natural for attention to drift, because it is hard for children to concentrate for long periods, even if they are interested in the story. Because this is especially true of younger children, it is advisable to keep the telling time for their stories to a minimum. In a longer story, watch to see if your listeners are maintaining eye contact with you or if some, especially at the outer edges of the group, are beginning to grow restless. If you are aware of these signs, you will be able to pull their attention back for the high points of the story. Remember these tips: maintain eye contact with as many people in the group as possible; let each person feel that you are telling the story to him or her.

Flexibility

If a child asks a question or makes a comment in the middle of a story, attempt to respond without breaking the flow of the story. For example, if a child asks practical questions about how long it took to get to Bethsaida or why the disciples brought so little food, the answer may be vague ("Oh, it took a long time"), or more specific ("Well, they didn't expect to have to feed all those people!"). Although questions should not be encouraged during the telling itself, when they do occur, it is important to acknowledge them.

The Ultimate Fear

What if I forget?

Try not to be upset, because it has happened to the best of storytellers. It is always appropriate to ask, "Now where was I?" or "Who was I talking about?" Not only does this keep the story moving, but it acknowledges that the listeners are participants in the storytelling event.

Discover your own style. One teller may have a flair for the dramatic, while another has a fairly matter-of-fact style, and still another is a quiet teller. Each can create the world of the story and touch the listener with its characters and events. The important thing is that your style of telling should be appropriate to the story, to your audience, and to you as a person. The best advice is to prepare thoroughly, relax, and enjoy the telling.

Storytelling Alternatives

Once you feel confident as a single storyteller, you may wish to attempt other more complicated forms of telling. A few alternatives are suggested here.

Dual Telling

In dual telling, there are two tellers. Usually one teller will present one character or set of characters, while the other presents the remainder. The tellers may take both the narration and the dialogue belonging to their characters. With a little practice, this can be an effective variation.

Story Participation

Story participation is a form of dual telling in which the children are invited to participate by taking the roles in the story.[3] It is an enjoyable technique for both the tellers and the children, and is similar to creative dramatics in activity and feeling.

Story Theater

Story theater is a form of group storytelling in which the story provides the scenario for a performance. No script is written. The performance is prepared through a series of games that develop skill in speaking, listening, imagination, movement, and the ability to play creatively as a group. One important company of story-theater performers is the Young

"Meeting with" the Bible Through Storytelling

People's Company, part of The Piven Theatre Workshop in Evanston, Illinois. The Young People's Company is a group of youths fourteen through seventeen years of age, who work under the direction of Joyce and Byrne Piven, pioneers in story theater. This is a highly complex technique and, though it is a delight to watch, takes considerable training.

Summary

Most tellers may never participate in the complete range of storytelling activities. Even so, each teller can continue to develop skill and confidence. In this way, children in each community can meet with the Bible persons and events, as they hear the ancient voices and imagine the ancient faces of such people as Abraham, Ruth, Joseph, the prophets, and Jesus. Through your telling, they will come to know the stories shared by Christians in all ages and places.

5.
"Responding out of" the Bible with Dance*

Moving one's body rhythmically in order to show emotion has been a natural means of expression for thousands of years. The Bible records that the early Hebrews danced to show their feelings of joy and sorrow, praise and pain. In II Samuel 6:14, it is recorded that when the ark was brought to Jerusalem, "David danced before the Lord with all his might." In Psalm 149:1-3, the people are admonished to "sing to the Lord a new song . . . praise his name with dancing," and in Psalm 150:3-6, we find:

> Praise him with trumpet sound;
>   praise him with lute and harp!
> Praise him with timbrel and dance;
>   praise him with strings and pipe!
> Praise him with sounding cymbals;
>   praise him with loud clashing cymbals!
> Let everything that breathes praise the Lord!
>   Praise the Lord!

With skillful and sensitive guidance, dance is an appropriate way to respond to encounters with the biblical text. Because it allows children to use their bodies, their feelings, and their imaginations, as well as their minds, it can help them express meanings that would be impossible with

---

*Written by Carol Johnson and Dorothy Jean Furnish.

words alone. The more intense the "feeling-into" activity has been, the more free and able children will be to "respond out of" the Bible text in creative ways. (In this chapter, we are using dance for a particular purpose—response; it also can be used for "feeling into," in much the same way as creative drama, described in chapter 3.)

While dance is not the easiest way to help children respond to biblical material, it is not something to fear, either. Before you use dance with children, you will need to do three basic things: (1) carefully introduce them to dance as a method of learning and expression; (2) be sure that dance is an appropriate way to respond to the Bible text at hand; and (3) develop a teaching plan.

Introducing Children to the Idea of Dance

Children are natural dancers! Watch small children when they hear music. Unless restrained by adults or lack of space, their bodies will instinctively move in rhythm with the beat. They clap, skip, jump, stretch, twirl, stand on tiptoe and fall to the ground. Unfortunately, by the time children reach elementary school, they have learned that such spontaneity is not an acceptable form of behavior, so when indoors and in the presence of adults, they limit their impulses to wiggling, and finally to politely "sitting still." Nevertheless, when out-of-doors and free from restrictions, they return to expressive and exuberant movement.

Since the church school setting is both inside the building and supervised by adults, some of the learned restraints will need to be removed before children will feel free to use their bodies in an expressive way. You may need to work on this for several weeks before you plan to have your first experience with dance as a response.

When to Introduce the Idea

When introducing the idea of dance to children, you may be able to take advantage of various church school settings. If you plan to use it in a church school session, you might begin your introduction four to six weeks ahead of time by scheduling five minutes at each session. Or, vacation church school will allow more time, perhaps twenty to thirty minutes, for introduction activities. Another possibility would be to use larger blocks of time during the Sunday school hour for one or two weeks. But whatever you do, you will need to consider your individual class and how the preparation time will fit into the purpose of the unit you are teaching.

How to Introduce the Idea

There are many ways to help children feel free to express themselves through creative movement. Some time before you plan to use dance as a way to respond to the Bible text, try some of these activities.

1. Follow-the-leader. Children line up as if to play the usual game of follow-the-leader. Ask the leader to concentrate on moving just one or two parts of the body—for example, just head and elbows. All the other children will try to follow, using as much of the available space as possible, and trying to make the movements flow smoothly through the space. After a minute or so, choose another leader, and focus on other parts of the body, perhaps this time the knees and fingers.

2. Imaginary Baseball. Have children take positions for a game of imaginary baseball. As they play, encourage them to make the movements as big and flowing as they possibly can. They can create a whole series of dance movements, one

for each position on the team. This activity is well-received by girls and boys who enjoy sports.

3. Balloons in the Air, Always. Divide the class into groups of four, providing two balloons for each group. The purpose of the game is to keep the balloons in the air as long as possible by batting them with various parts of the body. This can also be done as one large group.

These first three activities focused on freeing children to use all parts of their bodies. The next three are concerned with helping children not only to move without inhibition, but also to express specific emotions through movement.

4. "-ing" and "-ly" Words. Make two sets of flash cards: one set with "-ing" words such as running, jumping, skipping, falling, hopping, and walking; a second set with "-ly" words such as happily, sadly, angrily, lightly, energetically, and timidly. Choose two words, one from each set, call them out to the class, and let the children dance their interpretation.

5. Mood Music. Choose a piece of music with an obvious mood, such as "joy." Ask the children to show by the way they move how the music makes them feel. Play "sad" music as a contrast and once again ask them to show how they feel. Later they will be ready to interpret music that portrays more subtle and varied moods.

6. Crepe Paper. Give children long scarves or streamers of crepe paper as a variation when using mood music or "-ing" and "-ly" words. Props such as these help children feel less inhibited, since they can give their attention to the object and not to themselves.

When children have caught the idea that "inside feelings" can be expressed by "outside body movement," they are ready to respond to biblical passages through dance.

To arrive at this point may take several sessions during which activities such as those described are used.

How to Know If Dance Is an Appropriate Method of Response

Before the moment when you ask yourself, "Shall I experiment with dance as a response to this Bible passage?" there are certain conditions that already will have been met. You will know that the children have been introduced to the idea of dance, either in school experiences or in previous class experiences under your guidance, and that their response has been positive. Furthermore, you will have prepared your church school teaching plan and will know what "feeling-into" and "meeting-with" activities are going to be used. Now you are ready to ask if dance might be a way you can lead the children in response. Here are some criteria that might determine your answer.

1. If a feeling about the Bible passage is the important response, then dancing is appropriate, because through dance, feelings difficult to put into words can be captured and expressed.

2. If the "feeling-into" or "meeting-with" activities were intense enough to produce a strong mood, then dance may be considered. If strong feelings have not been created by the time the Bible text has been presented, probably there will not be enough feeling to support the use of dance as a way to respond.

3. If feelings are clearly present but are jumbled, and children are unable to articulate them, dance may be a useful activity; feelings that cannot be expressed verbally can sometimes be sorted out through dance. Opportunity to move and to talk with their bodies may help them discover their feelings.

Development of a Teaching Plan

The teaching plan is the third major task in helping children "respond out of" the Bible through dance. The planning process can be divided into four steps: (1) warm-ups as "feeling-into" activities; (2) "meeting with" the Bible passage; (3) dance as a response; (4) concluding the session.

Warm-Ups as "Feeling-into" Activities

The "feeling-into" activity is an ideal time to involve children in warm-ups. Bodies and imaginations can be limbered up at the same time. For example, children may be asked to imagine that they are having a snowball fight; some are throwers and others are targets. Targets are not allowed to run away, but must stay in one place. After a few minutes, children may change roles. Then the story of Stephen may be told—a man who, instead of snowballs, had stones thrown at him, and whose only crime was that he was a Christian.

Or, children may be asked to imagine they are in jail, tied so that they are unable to move. When they awake from sleep they discover that mice have chewed through their ropes, and they are free! They rub their wrists and ankles, stretch to hasten the return of circulation to their numbed bodies, and finally try to find a way out of the prison. This can be followed by the story of Paul, who was freed from prison chains by an earthquake. In both instances, the warm-up activities that encourage free body movement also call forth emotions that will add significance when the stories are heard.

"Meeting with" the Bible Passage

The Bible text may be presented in any of the ways described in chapter 2. Perhaps the most simple and effective way would be through storytelling.

Dance as a Response

Now that the children have "felt into" the story and "met with" it, they are ready to be encouraged to move freely and creatively in response to those feelings. There are four steps the children can be led to follow naturally as they express their feelings through dance.[1]

1. Grasp the idea with the imagination. Children have been helped to do this through the warm-up activities and the telling of the story.

2. Play Statues. Ask the children to show with a stationary body posture how the story has made them feel, or how they think some person in the story may have felt. For example, "Become a statue and show me how you imagine Stephen looked and felt when the people to whom he preached threw stones at him." Or, "Become a statue and show me how you felt when you heard that Paul and the other prisoners did not try to escape."

3. Move in place. Now, let the children move and twist their bodies without leaving their places, in order to show even more how they or the person in the story felt. Encourage them to extend their bodies in all directions, making the "statue" bigger, or to contract their bodies, making the "statue" smaller. Bigger and smaller, bigger and smaller, always moving smoothly from one size to the other, and always keeping the feelings they seek to portray vividly in their imaginations.

4. Move to another place. Children are now ready to move to other spots in the room, repeating these actions. Encourage them to change their locations slowly and with flowing motions, so as not to interrupt the rhythms they have established. As they reach their new places, they may want to express different emotions. A background of appropriate

recorded music will help the children discover smooth and rhythmic patterns of movement.

Ways to Conclude the Session

The final part of the plan is to discover a suitable way to conclude the experience. Here are five ways that have worked for others:

1. Recall feelings. Ask the children to recall the strongest feeling they had as they danced in response to hearing the Bible story. They might then be encouraged to do one last movement to express that feeling.

2. Use round-robin storytelling. Retell the story in a round-robin fashion. The children should be seated in a circle; one person starts the story, the next adds to it, and so on, until everyone has had at least one turn, and the story is finished. This activity helps children relate the dance back to the story in an intentional way. It also gives them the opportunity to talk about any new insights they may have discovered about the passage through the experience of the dance.

3. Use worship. Ask the group to sit in a circle on the floor, clasping hands with the persons on either side of them. Lead them in thanking God, either silently or aloud, for the time shared in dance, and for the gift of movement God has given.

4. Review with the children how this experience fits into the lesson purpose for the day.

5. Reread the passage directly from the Bible.

And so the plan has been completed, starting with warm-ups that stimulated their imaginations, moving on to an experience of the Bible text itself, then to the dance portion of the session, and finally to a meaningful conclusion. With this plan in mind we now turn to the use of dance in relation to two specific Bible texts.

Plan I: Parable of the Lost Sheep (Luke 15:3-7)

The parable of the lost sheep is the story of a sheep that wanders away from the flock and of a concerned shepherd who searches to find it. It is with great joy that the sheep finally is found and guided home. Like the concerned shepherd, God cares about each person. An exploration and expression of feelings is an appropriate response to this story. Two emotions are thrown into sharp contrast. The story begins with sadness and loss and moves on to joy and recovery. It finally concludes in a mood of praise and thanksgiving when it is realized that God is much like a concerned shepherd. Most children are not able to theologize about "joy in heaven" but they do know how happy they feel when they find a treasured object that has been lost, and they are able to feel awe and wonder as they catch a glimpse of what God is like.

√ *A "Feeling-into" Warm-Up*

Ask the children to stand up and find a space where they will be able to move freely. Encourage them to imagine they are sheep, grazing on a hillside covered with beautiful green grass. They are very, very small sheep. They run and jump and enjoy the warm sunshine overhead and the cool grass beneath their feet. Wherever they go they are careful to watch the shepherd (the teacher) because they know that getting lost is the worst thing that can happen to little sheep. Finally, when they have eaten enough, they fall fast asleep.

As the children follow the lead of your voice, a kind of follow-the-leader will take place. Through this activity their bodies have been prepared for movement about the room and their imaginations have been stimulated so that they are prepared to hear the story.

√ *"Meeting with" the Bible Passage*

Gently "awaken the sheep," and gather them in a group around you.

"One day Jesus told a story about a sheep that wandered away from the rest of the flock and really did get lost."

You now have the rapt attention of a captive audience for your telling of the story.

√ *Dance as a Response*

Ask the children to become "statues" showing how it feels to be lost. Then encourage the "statues" to move in place, now showing how it feels to be found! Let the children repeat this change several times as they begin to feel the rhythm of lost-to-found. Next, suggest that they move about the room, perhaps expressing "lost" in one spot and moving smoothly to other places in the room to show the feeling of "found." After the pattern has been established, mood music will help with the flow of the dance.

√ *Conclude the Session*

Help the children use words to tell how it feels to be found after being lost, and close with a prayer of thanks that God cares about each person just as the shepherd cared about each sheep.

Plan II: Psalm 150

Stories are not the only Bible passages suitable for use with children. Because of their vivid imagery, many of the psalms have an appeal for children, especially Psalm 150. The emotions of joy, praise, and exuberance that characterize this psalm are feelings with which most children can identify easily. It calls forth the same mood as that found in Psalm 100, which most children are eager to express: "Make a joyful noise . . ."

√ *A "Feeling-into" Warm-Up*

Distribute rhythm instruments to the children, and ask them to follow your directions.

"Make happy sounds with the triangles. Make happy sounds with the sticks."

Continue until all children have had a chance to participate. You may also combine some.

"Make a happy sound with cymbals and sticks."

Then make your final suggestion.

"Move around the room and show happy feelings with your instrument and with your whole body."

√ *"Meeting with" the Bible Passage*

Ask the children to sit in a circle with their rhythm instruments on the floor in front of them. Then say that there is a song in the Bible that tells how the Hebrew people used instruments to praise God. You may want to show sketches of the unique instruments they used in those days. Read the psalm from the Bible, and then reread it, this time substituting the instruments of the rhythm band collection for the biblical instruments. As the rhythm instrument version is read, let each child, at the mention of his or her instrument, make a joyful noise to the Lord!

"Responding out of" the Bible with Dance

√ *Dance as a Response*

Remind the children that the psalmist says "Let everything that breathes praise the Lord." Ask them to hold their instruments quietly, and to find a place in the room where they can move about without touching anyone else.

"Look at your instrument and do your very best to hold your body so that you and your instrument look alike."

You will want to enjoy with the children the hilarity this may create!

"Now move your body and play your instrument at the same time in a way that shows you are joyful. Move and play in time with the music."

Any happy, rhythmic music enhances the feeling of joy.

√ *Conclude the Session*

Gather the children in a circle again with rhythm instruments on the floor in front of them. Read Psalm 150 from the Bible and ask them to say it along with you. The psalm is short enough that if repeated in this way two or three times, most children will have memorized it by the end of the session.

Concluding Tips for Teacher

In addition to mastering the basic principles presented in this chapter, there are some very practical things you can do right away.

Begin to develop a collection of props: brightly colored scarves, crepe paper streamers, rhythm instruments, and balloons.

Make a set of large and easily read flash cards on which are written "-ing" and "-ly" words.

Start a music resource bank. On individual cassette tapes, record short bits of music, each expressing a different emotion—music that is sad, happy, carefree, lilting, angry, or peaceful. Also create tapes that contain music of contrasting moods on one tape—for example, a tape on which sad music becomes happy music, and another that would help children move from angry feelings to a mood of serenity.

Above all, avoid the temptation to "show off" the dances the children have created. This may be possible later, if a group grows enthusiastic about dancing and wants to share with others; but to suggest performance too early is sure to result in some children "freezing up" rather than being "freed up"! Just as in creative drama, the process is more important than the product.

6.
"Responding out of" the Bible in Word and Deed

The motto "Be ye doers of the word, and not hearers only" (James 1:22 KJV), framed and prominently displayed, used to be a permanent part of every Sunday school room in the junior department (grades four, five, and six). Unfortunately, the word "only" was often overlooked, with the result that this motto seemed to suggest that acting is a greater virtue than listening, and that one who listens is not involved in a meaningful activity. In an attempt to emphasize the necessity of action, the value of talking and listening sometimes has been slighted. However, when persons actually have experienced the events of the Bible, both words and deeds can be action responses.

Discussion as Response

As human beings, we are distinguished from other creatures by our ability to invent and use language in both its spoken and written forms. Although body gestures can express many messages, it is through words that highly complex communication is possible. When communication is one-way, from teacher to child, it is called the lecture method. Communication between teacher and student is the discussion method.

Discussion might seem to be the least controversial teaching method, but it does not have total acceptance. Those who prefer the lecture approach often refer to discussion as a "pooling of ignorance." Others, who understand the need for children to be physically active, deplore time spent in what seems a passive activity. These criticisms stem not so much from a disagreement with the method itself as from the way it has been used.

Before the Discussion

There are four conditions which need to be present in order for discussion to be an effective way for teachers, parents, and children to respond to an experience of the Bible.

1. In order for discussion to be meaningful, there must have been an experience worth responding to. If the "feeling-into" and "meeting-with" activities have been carried out so that the Bible has really "gotten into the child," there will be a rich experience from which the child can respond. If not, the discussion will be superficial.

2. Even when the response activity is a discussion, it first needs to be at the feeling level. Often, we have treated biblical content as so many facts to be learned and repeated back to the teacher, rather than as an experience to be felt and expressed. We told the story of the Last Supper, and then led a discussion that went something like this:

Teacher:	How many disciples were at the Last Supper?
Child:	Twelve.
Teacher:	Good. What were their names?
Children:	(Names are given with a good deal of prompting by the teacher.)
Teacher:	Which disciple was not loyal to Jesus?
Children:	(in chorus) Judas!

Teacher:	Fine! That is right! What was Judas going to do?
Child:	Betray Jesus.
Teacher:	All right. But why did he want to do that?
Child:	For money.
Teacher:	Yes, but for how much money?
Child:	Thirty pieces of silver.
Teacher:	Do you know how much money that would be today?

And so the interchange would go, on and on. Having drawn from the children all the right answers, the teacher concluded that they now knew the story.

But this sense of satisfaction was ill-founded. In this "lesson" there was no recognition of the anxiety the disciples felt about the growing animosity toward Jesus. Nor was there any room for the sorrow and guilt they must have felt when confronted with the thought that one of their own number would betray him. There was no sensitivity to the contrast between values—money or a life. And least of all was there any opportunity for the children to respond with their own feelings about the impending death of an innocent and good man.

When the Bible is taught only as a series of factual right-or-wrong statements, it loses the power to capture a child's imagination and emotions. Commitment to become a follower of Jesus is not prompted by facts about an event, but by feelings about a person.

3. If response to the Bible is to be discussion, both adults and children should share meanings and feelings, both should ask questions, and both should be active listeners.

Serious responses should be considered seriously. Teachers who answer children with verbal or nonverbal language that says, "What a stupid comment!" should not be surprised when their further efforts at discussion prove unsatisfactory.

Many discussions are ineffective because adults respond to what they want to hear, rather than to what is actually being said. When children are conditioned to make certain responses, they may articulate the adult's response to the Bible text; they do not express their own reactions—they only express their desire to please the adult.

When children are helped to express their feelings about the Bible, a dialogue that reflects meaning is more apt to occur. Using this approach, a discussion of the Last Supper might sound like this:

Teacher:	How do you feel about the story of Jesus eating supper with his disciples for the last time?
Child:	The supper was all right, but I didn't like the way it ended.
Teacher:	What do you mean, about the ending?
Child:	Well, that one of the disciples was a traitor. That made me sad.
Teacher:	That makes me sad, too. I've often wondered how the disciples felt when Jesus said one of them was going to betray him.
Child:	They probably wondered who it was.
Child:	They were probably afraid he meant them!
Child:	I think they must have been angry!
Teacher:	The disciples must have had a lot of

| | mixed-up feelings. I hadn't thought about them being angry, though. |
| Child: | Well, *I'd* have been angry! Why did people want to kill Jesus? It wasn't fair! |

The secret of teaching dialogically is the ability of the teacher to be present fully with the child.

4. When discussion is chosen as the way to help children respond to the Bible, the conversation should be kept within the limits of their intellectual ability. Often discussions end in failure and problems with discipline, not because children are inherently naughty, but because the conversation has left their concrete world and has taken on an abstraction to which they cannot relate.

"Why did people want to kill Jesus? It wasn't fair!" That is a question children can and want to discuss, because being fair is one of childhood's highest values. Attempts to discuss such abstract concepts as "suffering servant" and "atonement" are better left for their youth and adult years.

Summary

Whether or not children have learned the facts of a Bible text may be discovered by involving them in a discussion of the story, but discussion can achieve other results that are even more important. Through discussion children can be helped to respond to the Bible honestly, at both the feeling level and the intellectual level. They can catch a sense of what it means to be members of the Christian community as they engage in serious reflection with the teachers and with one another about a significant part of the community's tradition. When their responses, however immature and fragmentary, have been taken seriously, they will be willing to share their thoughts again in the future.

Service Projects as Response

Churchwide service projects are traditional at special seasons of the year; they may be initiated as part of a denominational or ecumenical program, or they may be in response to some immediate need. At these times children's groups are often asked to join in the total church effort. It is not always necessary to relate the project to a Bible story or text. It is enough to help children understand that the service project is the Church at work.

Although most service projects do not originate as a result of Bible study, some may, if concern for others and the desire to be of service seems the most appropriate response, and it is those projects we will discuss here.

Before You Initiate a Service Project

"Let's do a service project!" is more apt to be the spontaneous response to a "meeting with" the Bible if three conditions are present.

1. The Bible selection should have within it a challenge to service, if we expect children to respond in that way. For example, the "As you did it to one of the least of these" passage (Matthew 25:34-45) calls for a service response much more than does the Twenty-third Psalm.

2. An already established atmosphere of caring and social action within the church or home will prompt children to think of service. If children have not seen the church or their parents at work for others, they are unlikely to respond to a Bible passage by suggesting such an action.

3. Older children are more likely to respond to Bible study by suggesting service. Service projects are most appropriate for younger children when there is an actual need that they can see. If children are personally acquainted

with flood victims in their community, there is no need for a biblical rationale for service. Serving others is what Christians do. But the mental operations required to go from an ancient writing to a present-day meaning, and finally to an implication for action, can be performed only by older children, and even then with some difficulty.

When the atmosphere is supportive and the biblical text appropriate, older children may find a project of service to others the most natural response to make. For times like this, here are some specific suggestions.

Whatever the response children make, it should come from within their own feelings and understandings. If in your planning you think a service project would be a fitting response, the "feeling-into" and "meeting-with" phases of the lesson plan will need to be carefully prepared. Children may agree to a service project, but unless it is a spontaneous response, they may not have enough interest to complete it. When a project must be completed by the teachers, it is a sign that it was not really the children's project in the first place.

A decision to do a service project is unique. Other responses are open-ended. That is, a wide range of ideas and emotions can be expressed through dance, art, or discussion. To propose painting one's feelings is not to say what those feelings ought to be; it is only to suggest a way to express them. A service project, on the other hand, assumes not only that children have feelings, but that they have a particular feeling—a concern for others.

To avoid manipulating the responses of children, the decision to begin a service project should be preceded by thorough discussion. If the course of the discussion seems to warrant it, the teacher might ask, "What if we, right here in this church, took this Bible passage seriously? Is there anything we might do?" If there are no enthusiastic answers, it is obvious that for this group of children, a service project is not a natural response. But if ideas begin to flow, then such a project may be considered.

These questions will help you and your class choose a project: Does this project meet a real need? What would it mean in terms of time, skills, and money? Are we willing and able to put forth as much effort as will be needed? To obtain answers, the class may need to do some research. They may want to involve their parents or other church and community adults. When all the facts are in, the decision can be made.

Keeping the Project a Response to the Bible

A service project as a response to the Bible points in two directions. First, it points forward toward those it seeks to serve. It is a concrete action that meets a tangible need. It also points backward to the Bible passage itself, as it helps to reinforce the significance of the story for the children. For this reason it is important to maintain a link to the Bible passage until the project has been completed. Here are some ways this might be done.

1. Suggest that the children name the project to remind them of the Bible story—"The Inasmuch Project," "The Good Sam Club," or "The Second Milers."

2. Guide a committee of children in making a bulletin board on which they post appropriate Bible story pictures and pictures of the project as it progresses.

3. Help the children choose one phrase or verse from the Bible passage, and make a banner to be displayed in the classroom until the project is completed.

Concluding the Project

Several weeks may elapse between the Bible study and the completion of the project. Choose a way to conclude that will help the children recall the fun they had together as they worked on the project, and that will at the same time emphasize the importance of what they have accomplished. Perhaps you will plan a worship service or a party-type celebration. Guests may be invited who will share in reflecting on the events surrounding the project. Also included should be a recall of the Bible text that underlay the project.

Summary

A service project is one of the most complex responses children can make to a Bible passage. Thoughtful discussion should precede its selection; children should value it as their own choice; both need and practicability should be considered; and it should be followed through to a meaningful conclusion.

7.
How to Plan

You want children to think of the Bible as their book. In order to do this you are convinced that the Bible needs to be a part of the child's own life. And you want children to experience the Bible, rather than simply knowing it as facts about people in the past. The three guidelines of "feeling into," "meeting with," and "responding out of" the Bible sound helpful. Where to begin?

If you are full of ideas and eager to start, you may want to omit this chapter. On the other hand, if you are sure of your destination, but you still feel a need for a road map, this chapter is for you.

You may want to develop your own instructional strategies/plan of procedure for a session or a unit, with a Bible reference as your only guide. In that case your question will be, "How can the guidelines help me plan, when I have to depend completely on my own resources?"

Most of you, however, will be working with instructional materials that have been provided for your use. In this case your question will be, "How can I use the three guidelines to adapt the instructional plans I have been given?"

Here are suggestions for the use of the three guidelines in lesson preparation: first, when you have only a Bible reference to work from; and second, when you are adapting a suggested lesson plan.

Beginning with Bible Text Only

Those most likely to start with only a Bible passage are the persons who write the instructional materials. If you should find yourself without such resources, then you can follow this procedure and write your own instructional plans.

Let us assume that you want to teach the story of the children of Israel being led out of bondage by Moses.

Step One: Discover Possible Emphases and Choose One

Over the years, Bible texts have come to have certain meanings attached to them, but further thought may reveal other implications. To discover the full richness of a passage, follow this plan. First, read the Bible text and reflect on its importance to you. Do you find parallels in your own life? Next, read about the passage in a Bible commentary. What have biblical scholars discovered about its authorship, the age in which it was written, the intended audience, and its probable meaning? Finally, try to imagine what significance children may find in it.

As a result of your study and reflection, select one or more themes that you have discovered are valid in terms of your personal experience, the best of biblical scholarship, and the understanding level of the children. For example, in the story of Moses, these are some aspects of the story that might be emphasized.

1. God is always present.
2. Moses was a great leader.
3. Never give up a dream.
4. God will free the oppressed.

Begin to develop a planning chart. Choose one of the emphases, remembering that the others can be found in the text and may be cited by the children. We will assume that you have chosen "God will free the oppressed."

PLANNING CHART

Step One	Step Two	Step Three	Step Four
Emphasis	"Feeling-into" Activity	"Meeting-with" Activity	"Respond-ing-out-of" Activity
1. God is present			
2. Moses a leader			
3. persever-ance			
4. *God will free the op-pressed*			

Step Two: Discover Possible "Feeling-into" Activities and Choose One

To help children "feel into" the story, it is necessary to identify the feelings of the Bible characters. Ask yourself, "How did the oppressed people in the story feel? Frightened? Angry? Discouraged and resentful?" Then ask, "What activities can children engage in that will help them feel these emotions?" Several possibilities may come to mind.

1. Creative drama—help children imagine themselves as oppressed people.
2. Art—ask children to show through painting and other art forms how it feels to be angry or frightened or discouraged.
3. Discussion—help children recall times when they were angry, frightened, discouraged, or resentful.

88

How to Plan

Choose an activity that is suitable to your space and your ability, and that provides variety and a chance for the children to experience the story of Moses. Creative drama is an effective method.

PLANNING CHART

Step One	Step Two	Step Three	Step Four
Emphasis	"Feeling-into" Activity	"Meeting-with" Activity	"Respond-ing-out-of" Activity
God will free the oppressed	1. creative drama 2. art 3. discussion		

Step Three: Discover Possible "Meeting-with" Activities and Choose One

Ask yourself, "What are some ways the children can 'meet with' the story of Moses that will help them feel they are actually participants in the event?" These are only a few of the possible ways.

1. See a motion picture about Moses.
2. Listen to someone tell the Moses story.
3. Hear a taped dramatization of the story of Moses.

When Bible texts are difficult to "feel into," the "meeting with" must be as exciting and involving as possible. In the Moses account, however, the use of creative drama has such power that a simple, straightforward telling of the story is appropriate.

PLANNING CHART

Step One	Step Two	Step Three	Step Four
Emphasis	"Feeling-into" Activity	"Meeting-with" Activity	"Respond-ing-out-of" Activity
God will free the oppressed	*creative drama*	1. motion picture 2. *story-telling* 3. drama on tape	

Step Four: Discover Possible "Responding-out-of" Activities and Choose One

Ask, "In the light of the emphasis I have chosen, and the 'feeling-into' activity I have planned, what response from the children might I expect?" You will want to have several activities in mind, so that you can choose the one most appropriate to the mood of the group.

1. Dance how the story made them feel.
2. Discuss who the oppressed are today.
3. Dramatize the story again.
4. Service project—do something for the oppressed.

The spontaneous response of one group of girls and boys was to dramatize the story again, this time speaking the parts themselves instead of moving in response to the words of a narrator. If you wish to encourage your class members to do this, include it on your planning chart.

PLANNING CHART

Step One	Step Two	Step Three	Step Four
Emphasis	"Feeling-into" Activity	"Meeting-with" Activity	"Respond-ing-out-of" Activity
God will free the op-pressed	*creative drama*	*story-telling*	1. dance 2. discussion 3. *dramatize story again* 4. service project

You have created the heart of a lesson plan by choosing one of the themes you discovered in your study of the biblical text and by selecting one activity for each of the three guidelines. But you could have chosen other patterns and sequences. Through the use of the planning chart above and the possibilities projected there, forty-eight different lesson plans could be created for this one study of Moses!

Adapting Ready-Made Lesson Plans

Seldom will you need to begin your planning without the help of printed resources, but you may want to adapt the resources to fit the approach of this book. Here is one way to begin the task of adapting a ready-made session plan.

Step One: Discover the Emphasis

The purpose of the session has already been stated in your teacher's guide by the writer, and the chosen biblical references will support that theme. You will want to stay with this emphasis, since it is a vital part of your church's overall educational objective, and since it is part of a total curriculum plan. When you discover the emphasis, write it in column 1 of your planning chart.

Step Two: "Feeling-into" Activities

Study your teacher's guide to find the suggested "feeling-into" activities, although they will probably not be labeled that way. You are looking for activities that will help children identify with the emotions experienced by persons mentioned in the Bible passage, or emotions that the Bible text may appropriately call out of the children themselves. Write these activities in column 2 of your planning chart. If you do not find any "feeling-into" activities, leave the column empty.

Step Three: "Meeting-with" Activities

Study your teacher's guide to find the suggested ways to present the biblical text. Often it will recommend that you read or tell the story. Write these in column 3 of your planning chart.

Step Four: "Responding-out-of" Activities

Study your teacher's guide to find the suggested "responding-out-of" activities. The most common response activity will be discussion. If you find none, leave the space blank.

Step Five: Complete Planning Chart

Taking into consideration the theme suggested and the degree of involvement in the "meeting-with" activities, fill in any blanks on the chart with as many alternatives as you can think of. Even where some activities have been suggested by your teacher's guide, you are free to add others.

Step Six: Finalize Plans

You are now ready to outline your session. Choose one activity each from columns two, three, and four, and begin to gather the necessary supplies. Complete your plans by inserting announcements, offering, and worship at suitable places. Often the response activity will become part of the worship time.

Summary: A Practice Run

Now that you have in mind the basic idea of using the three guidelines in lesson planning, fill in the blanks in the following planning charts for the indicated Bible passages (these passages have been used as examples in other chapters). Then prepare a sample lesson plan. You will need a Bible, a Bible commentary, and perhaps a concordance.

If you have problems, you may want to reread chapter 2, "Three Guidelines." For other practical help, read the last chapter, "Next Steps."

FEEDING THE FIVE THOUSAND

Emphasis	"Feeling-into" Activity	"Meeting-with" Activity	"Respond-ing-out-of" Activity
1.	1.	1. story-telling	1.
2.	2.		2.
3.	3.		3.

MY LESSON PLAN

PARABLE OF THE LOST SHEEP

Emphasis	"Feeling-into" Activity	"Meeting-with" Activity	"Respond-ing-out-of" Activity
1.	1.	1.	1. dance
2.	2.	2.	
3.	3.	3.	

MY LESSON PLAN

Living the Bible with Children

PSALM 150

Emphasis	"Feeling-into" Activity	"Meeting-with" Activity	"Responding-out-of" Activity
1.	1.	1.	1. dance
2.	2.	2.	
3.	3.	3.	

MY LESSON PLAN

96

THE GOOD SAMARITAN

Emphasis	"Feeling-into" Activity	"Meeting-with" Activity	"Respond-ing-out-of" Activity
1.	1.	1.	1. service project
2.	2.	2.	
3.	3.	3.	

MY LESSON PLAN

8.
The Total-Environment Way of Teaching*

Chapter 7 explored a way to plan a session in which a single, distinct Bible story, such as a parable, could be taught. That planning approach assumed that the three guidelines, "feeling into," "meeting with," and "responding out of" would be used in that sequence for each session. It was also assumed that one teacher or a teaching team would direct the entire class of children through each of the three types of activities.

Perhaps at this point you find yourself saying, "This is fine as far as it goes—but my teaching team would rather use a learning-center approach. We want to develop a complete curriculum unit in such a way as to totally immerse our group of children in a cluster of events that tell a life story, such as Paul's life and journeys, or Jesus' life and ministry. We want them to really feel as though they were there. We want them to 'become' Paul and Timothy and Priscilla and to 'live' in Paul's world. And we want to let the children move independently and interact with us as teachers in a much more permissive and fluid way. How can we use the three guidelines to plan this kind of learning-center approach?"

If you have thoughts similar to these, this chapter is especially for you, because you and your teaching team are searching for a style called the total-environment way of teaching. This is experiential teaching at its best. It draws

*Written by Mary Jo Osterman.

upon the whole range of children's senses, feelings, and imaginations. It also makes use of their limited but developing mental abilities. In invites them to become totally involved in learning.

"Total environment" means creating a particular physical setting in your classroom. If your unit is about Joseph and his brothers, the setting becomes the biblical environment of Canaan in Joseph's time. Several life-size scenes are set up around the room to depict Joseph's home, the pastures with the pit, and the caravan of the Midianite traders. These scenes are ministage settings in which the children work and play. As the unit progresses, the scenes change to those of Egypt. By offering this kind of physical environment, your teaching team can in some sense transport your children back to biblical times and places. You can create a new "where" for them so that when they walk into their classroom they feel as if they are walking into the land of Joseph. In other units, they can walk into the town of Nazareth or into the world of Paul's travels. Although this chapter generally refers to biblical environments, the idea can be extended to church history units and to some contemporary themes in the curriculum units, as well.

"Total environment" also means creating the biblical characters who originally peopled the ministages you have set up in your classroom. Again, if your unit is about Joseph, the teachers will take on some of the roles: Joseph; his brothers; his father, Jacob; his mother; the traders; the Pharaoh. You will dress in a costume, informally acting the part as you move around the learning center, and talk about the things your character might talk about as you interact with the other teachers and with the children. Through your costume, actions, and verbal and nonverbal interchanges, you can call forth from the children feelings, actions, and responses similar to those of the biblical people. The children will begin to respond in character to you, to the physical environment, and to one another. A child may slowly "become" Joseph, one of his brothers, his mother, his sister-in-law, or his niece.

The total-environment way of teaching might be called structured play or dramatic play. It is not the free play you have observed in nursery and kindergarten rooms. Nor is it a skit or drama developed from a written script. Rather, structured play lies somewhere in-between. You and your teaching team will have firmly in mind the cluster of events telling the life story of an important biblical character. Based on your understandings of that life story, you will provide the scenes, the props, and the activities for the children. You will also have that life story in mind as you informally play the roles of the biblical characters with the children. Therefore, you and your children will "play" the story within the structure you, as the teachers, provide. In the world of theater, this structured play is sometimes called improvisation in an environment.

Activities that help children "feel into," "meet with," and "respond out of" the biblical story are essential to the total-environment way of teaching. But they do not occur in the simple one-two-three sequence for each class session, as described in the previous chapter. The total-environment way of teaching is an excellent example of the axiom that "the whole is greater than the sum of the parts."

The following section is offered to describe how one teaching team slowly developed the total-environment way with a group of first- and second-graders as they taught them about Jesus' life and ministry. Later in the chapter, the approach will be analyzed and a way to plan for it will be presented. Just now, relax and get the feel of the whole approach. Try to imagine yourself as one of the teachers.

The Total-Environment Way of Teaching

We Lived the Story

This is how one younger elementary teaching team planned from Advent to Easter to the Modern Church.

The curriculum for our first and second graders outlined eighteen Sundays—from Advent to Easter—on Jesus. And eight more on the church. Our teaching team was not sure it could be done. With units of only four to six weeks in length, the children's interest had wavered. Little carry-over had occurred. How could these children ever experience the chronological flow of Jesus' life or grasp the meaning of the crucial events which brought the Christian church into being? But—we decided to try!

Experience was the key, we knew. The children's attention span as a group was about five minutes long. They ignored the book corner. They liked the mechanics of the projectors and record players, but we were not sure how much content they had learned. They loved to paint, to make things, to play, to do; but they were very shy about any activity which called upon them to perform.

Somehow, through paint, construction, play, and action, we needed to help them *experience* Jesus' birth, childhood, adulthood; his ministry, death, resurrection; and the beginnings of the Christian church. To achieve this goal would be to build a sound foundation for later serious study.

With this goal and the children in mind, our team began to plan. We agreed to change the room and activities frequently. We chose as sub-units:

Advent/Christmas (5 weeks)
Childhood Days (5 weeks)
Adulthood/Ministry (4 weeks)
Palm Sunday/Easter (3 weeks)
First Christians (3 weeks)

101

Our Church Gathers (4 weeks)
Our Church Reaches Out (2 weeks).

Advent/Christmas

On the first Sunday in Advent, the children were greeted with a sign which announced "Christmas Is Coming." In each corner of the room, the scene was set: an inn, a stable nearby, a shepherds' hillside, and a desert in a far corner. Each scene was labeled with a bright poster. And everywhere, the large yellow star shone.

Each Sunday a different part of the Christmas story was emphasized—through filmslip, song, verse, creche—and then "worked on" in the room. A manger was made; cows, donkeys, sheep, and camels painted. As the scenes came alive weekly, props were added, such as costumes, a baby doll, and shepherds' staffs.

An art worktable attracted some children with more developed muscle control (and some with too much inhibition to work in the large scenes). Art work corresponded to the emphasis of the morning.

Our theme song became "Hey! Hey! Anybody Listening?"[1] It was sung each Sunday with guitar and rhythm instruments.

The three teachers moved among the children to encourage their actions and conversations informally. We hoped for that spark which would kindle imaginations and overcome self-consciousness so the children could *really be* Mary and Joseph, the shepherds, wise men, and innkeeper. Halfhearted attempts were made, with teachers directing the pantomime, but real identification did not occur.

However, evaluation of this first sub-unit was positive: the children had somewhat experienced the birth event of Jesus' life. And the teachers had glimpsed a teaching style that could bring the Christian story alive for children.

The Total-Environment Way of Teaching

Childhood Days

With a quick change of scenery, children were next greeted by the sign—"And Jesus Grew." Our room had become the town of Nazareth, with Jesus' home, a marketplace, a synagogue, and a well-stocked carpenter's shop.

We introduced the Childhood Days sub-unit, and built on the Christmas unit, through the use of the song "And Jesus Grew"[2]:

> He was born and laid in a manger
> There were shepherds and kings who came,
> And he had around him a family,
> And Jesus grew.

> Now his father was Joseph, a carpenter
> And he worked with his tools and woods,
> And Mary cared for her infant son,
> And Jesus grew.

To our amazement, one child responded, "but Jesus was never a little boy like me—he didn't grow like me!" The faces of others indicated agreement: Jesus was different—maybe like Superman? Somehow we had to help these children experience Jesus as a growing child just like themselves.

As the children moved freely about the room, early Bible-time activities were suggested by word, by pictures, by art, and construction materials. Soon a large boat was being built; sandals, coins, and bowls were created; bread was baked and butter made; sand writing and scroll making were carried on and mezuzahs made. Scenery painting flourished everywhere.

Each Sunday we began with the song "And Jesus Grew," and composed our own verses about the children's activities. Soon we had added:

He went to the market with Joseph
They took coins—bronze, silver and gold,
And they bought a clay bowl and some sandals,
And Jesus grew.

Now he went to school at the synagogue;
He learned reading and writing there.
He prayed to God and he worshiped, too,
And Jesus grew.

He went to the priests at the Temple;
He listened so carefully.
He questioned them and thought on it.
And Jesus grew.

Informal conversations continued: "Let's finish this bread and go to the marketplace. I need some new sandals today." Teachers self-consciously stopped to "buy" a clay bowl with a bronze coin or became the seller in the marketplace. Some giggly, sporadic role-playing began to take place by the children also.

Each Sunday, the sessions ended in the synagogue with a brief worship in the Jewish style, lighting the four-wicked candle, reading verses from scrolls, saying *"Shalom"* and "the Lord bless and keep you."

Adulthood/Ministry

One Sunday in February, after four weeks immersion in childhood activities and life in a village, the children were greeted with a new sign "And Jesus Was Grown UP!" The room now held a seashore (with the boat tied up at water's edge), Mary and Martha's home, the Temple, and the marketplace.

The teaching team added a new member, a seminary student who agreed to "be" the grown-up Jesus. Wearing Christmas pageant robe and old sandals, he wandered around the room, engaged children in conversation, and told stories.

On the first Sunday of this sub-unit, "Jesus" was baptized by John the Baptist in the River Jordan (butcher paper rolled across the floor). Children were "baptized" in the river throughout the morning. Another Sunday, teachers acted out a playlet called "Jesus Visits Mary and Martha at Bethany" (a modern paraphrase by one of the teachers). Later, Jesus replayed the story with the children.

In the marketplace, buying and selling began in earnest. At the seashore, net-making was popular. A teacher in costume conversed about "this man Jesus who told stories and talked about loving our enemies and doing good." Jesus' disciples were introduced, and each child became one—except for several girls who decided to become Jesus' mother, or Elizabeth or Mary or Martha!

By this time we had added the next two verses to our song:

He went to the river Jordan.
He found John the Baptizer there;
And he said to John "Please baptize me."
And Jesus was Grown UP.

Jesus went to the seashore,
He saw boats and fishermen, too.
And he called and said "Come, follow me."
And Jesus was Grown UP.

One Sunday, conversation shifted toward a discussion of people who did not like Jesus. Jesus talked about taking a trip to Jerusalem.

Palm Sunday/Easter

Near the end of the session before Palm Sunday, butcher paper was rolled across the room to the Temple. Jesus gathered his disciples and friends for the trip. A crowd stood along the road and waved paper palm branches. Jesus walked the road, stopped to talk, waved. Everyone gathered at the Temple for worship and a new verse was added to our song:

> Jesus went to Jerusalem.
> The crowds were glad that he came.
> And they waved palm branches and sang
> "Hosanna."
> And Jesus was Grown UP.

On Palm Sunday the children distributed palm fronds in church. They sang "And Jesus Grew" for the congregation prior to the sermon, then returned to their learning center to continue "living" the story. Again, the Palm Sunday trip was played, this time with real palm fronds carefully "saved" from church! At the close of the session the last verse was introduced:

> Now Jesus had some enemies.
> They had him put to death.
> But on Easter Day his friends all know
> That Jesus Lives On!

The events of the coming passion week were discussed. The children attended church with their parents on Easter Sunday to celebrate the fact that "Jesus Lives On!"

The First Christians

After Easter, the room looked just the same, but "Jesus" was gone. Conversations changed: "Good News: Jesus is still alive." "Remember when Jesus told us the story about . . ." "The Roman soldiers questioned me in the marketplace today." "Let's meet tonight at Mary and Martha's, but be careful not to let anyone see you. Make the sign of the fish when you knock.''

The next Sunday, Mary and Martha's house had a fourth wall for a secret meeting place. A jail stood in another corner. A tunnel led to the catacombs (formerly the coatroom).

A teacher with guitar sang with the Christians who were put in jail by Roman soldiers. Christians painted on the walls about Jesus and God; non-Christians painted ''I hate Jesus.''

Wire fish symbols were worn by Christians to gain entrance to a night meeting, which was a hurried, silent meal of matzo crackers and grape juice. A disciple watched for soldiers who stomped the streets. The Christians stole silently across ''town'' to the catacombs for a secret worship meeting. (The role-playing came naturally; teachers guided by their own participation.)

At the end of one secret catacomb meeting a child read a scroll which announced that ''Emperor Constantine has become a Christian and now Christians do not have to hide anymore.'' A spontaneous cheer rose from the children hidden in the catacombs. Talk began about ''building our own church to worship in.''

Our Church Gathers—and Reaches Out

The following Sunday a new unit began with transition talk from ''being early Christians'' to ''being Christians today.'' The room now held a modern sanctuary, a choir room, a ''Great Hall'' for after-church coffee, a classroom, a minister's office. We ''played'' our church for six Sundays, and ended the spring with an open-house for parents, complete with short worship service and our own ''coffee time'' in our own ''Great Hall.''

We Lived "The Story"

From December through May, we lived the story of Jesus and the founding of the Christian church. Our beginning half-hearted role-playing efforts had borne fruit—the children had become Mary and Martha, Jesus and the disciples, the early Christians and the Roman soldiers! They had played and worked in Nazareth! They had fished and listened to Jesus by the seashore! They had waved and cheered by the roadside! They had feared in the jails and catacombs because they had tried to share the "good news" about Jesus! They had shouted their joy for the freedom to worship openly!

In retrospect, our team knows of times and places where we could have been more effective—but *we rejoice with our children that for six months we lived The Story of Our Christian Heritage.*

How Total Environment Uses the Three Guidelines

Now that you have a feel for the total-environment approach to teaching the Bible, we will look at the preceding example more closely. Use of each of the guidelines will be identified and discussed.

Guideline One: "Feeling into"

The first guideline, "feeling into," means somehow bringing to the surface in the child the same emotions as those felt by the biblical characters.

In the example, "feeling-into" activities are found in both dimensions of total environment—the physical environment and the role-playing by the teachers.

The physical environment of the room helped the children "feel into" the story of Jesus' life in an indirect way.

Children entered the ministages and worked on activities initially on the basis of their here-and-now interest in such things as painting, working with clay, or pounding nails into wood. These activities drew upon their senses and imaginations and feelings, to prepare them for experiencing some of the same emotions as the biblical people who had lived in those scenes. As children finished constructing the scenery for the ministages and entered into the other activities of that setting (such as net-making in the seashore scene), they began to "own" the scenes and to move into and live in them.

The second type of "feeling-into" activity involved the role-playing of the teachers. The children were able to make the scenes their own, mainly because of the teachers' informal portrayal of biblical characters in the midst of these scenes. The teachers' one-line verbal interactions helped the children connect their here-and-now interests and feelings with the past. For example, when a teacher, role-playing a new Christian, said, "The Roman soldiers questioned me in the marketplace today," that teacher was in effect "hooking" the children's feelings of fear and anxiety toward aggressive, authoritarian persons. The children were able to respond to this bit of the story with the same feelings, thoughts, and actions as those of a biblical person, because the feelings were familiar to them in their real world.

In keeping with the learning-center concept, the teaching team could have utilized a more direct style through the creation of a "time machine" at the classroom entrance, complete with flashing lights, dials, ringing bells and buzzers. As children arrived from home or worship service and entered the time machine, the teachers could have utilized specific motivational activities to help them feel the same emotions as the biblical people (see chapter 3, " 'Feeling into' the Bible Through Creative Drama"). The focus of these motivational activities would have been on the emotions of the various biblical characters the teachers wanted the children to become.

Guideline Two: "Meeting with"

The second guideline, "meeting with," refers to helping children encounter the text in an exciting and involving way. "Meeting with" means telling the biblical story in such a way that the child "hears" it. Many different methods of presenting or revealing the story may be used.

Three types of "meeting-with" activities can be identified in the example of total-environment teaching: formal, semiformal, and informal.

The formal ways of presenting the biblical story were preplanned by the teachers. These "meeting-with" activities included: the telling of the Christmas story in a different way at the beginning of each Advent session; the singing of "And Jesus Grew" at the beginning of each session during the childhood and adult units on Jesus' life; the role-playing by the teachers in the skit about Mary and Martha; the reading of the scroll about Constantine by the child in the catacombs.

The semiformal ways of presenting the story also were preplanned. However, these ways involved much improvisation on the part of teachers and children during the session: the wandering "Jesus" telling parables to the children; the parade on Palm Sunday; the hurried meal, followed by the silent stealing across town to the catacombs.

The informal ways of presenting the story were sometimes preplanned in a general sense, but more often they were spontaneous. Teachers improvised with the children both verbal and nonverbal interactions appropriate to the situations and in this way disclosed bits and pieces of the biblical story. Children also met with some of the story each time they walked into their classroom and absorbed the story revealed by the ministages.

Guideline Three: "Responding out of"

The third guideline, "responding out of," suggests that children should be given an opportunity to make some kind of response after they have "met with" the biblical story. These responses may be spontaneous feeling-and-acting responses, thinking responses, or intentional deciding-and-acting responses. The purpose of eliciting these responses is to help children discover and express biblical meanings.

In the example of total-environment teaching, two kinds of children's responses can be identified—thinking responses and spontaneous feeling-and-acting responses. There was no intentional decision-making leading to a service-type action.

Thinking responses occurred in several places. The children "met with" a portion of the biblical story of Jesus' life when the teachers sang the first two verses of the song "And Jesus Grew." The child's reaction was a thinking response: "But Jesus was never a little boy like me." Another kind of thinking response occurred when the teachers discussed the events of Passion Week with the children and briefly explored the significance of singing, "But on Easter Day his friends all know that Jesus lives on."

Spontaneous feeling-and-acting responses occurred throughout the various subunits on Jesus. When the two children who had worked hardest on the boat finally finished the sails and oars, they climbed into the boat, surveyed the room with smiles of satisfaction, then climbed out and went on to other activities. The children's silence during the secret meal and their sneaking across town to the catacombs were feelings translated into actions. So was the noisy aggressive

111

stomping of those children who became Roman soldiers. Feeling responses were also evident in the graffiti written on the walls of the jail. Finally, the spontaneous cheer of the Christians hidden in the catacombs was perhaps the ultimate indication that the children were feeling the emotions of the biblical characters and were responding from deep within themselves to the total environment of their classroom.

In another effort to elicit responses from the children, at the end of each session or subunit, the teaching team could have taken the children back into the time machine for a few minutes of debriefing. They could have explored with them the meanings the children had given to their experiences in the total-environment learning center. The four dimensions of meaning proposed in *Exploring the Bible with Children* could have served as a guide for the debriefing:

1. What does it mean to me, the child? Here children are encouraged to express what the activities of the learning center meant to them.

2. What does it mean to you, the teacher? Here the teacher shares his or her own understanding of the Bible, being careful that it is expressed in language children are able to understand.

3. What did it mean to them, the first-century Christians? Here children can use their imaginations to wonder how those people felt long ago.

4. What does it mean to us, the church today? Here is the time to explore what the text may be saying to the church as a gathered community.

In this discussion of the use of the three guidelines in total-environment teaching, it becomes clear that they do not occur in each session as a simple one-two-three sequence. Rather, the relationships between and among the guidelines are much more complex.

Within this total-environment approach, the guidelines become fluid processes, rather than three distinct types of activities with discernible beginnings and endings. "Feeling-into" moments occur many times for the children throughout the session. These times often flow into the "meeting-with" processes without distinguishable breaks. Finally, because they are moving and choosing freely, the children in the room are free to create their own responses at any time.

Steps for Planning the Total-Environment Approach

The total-environment way of teaching requires planning at three different levels: unit planning (at least three weeks prior to teaching); subunit planning (at least two weeks prior to teaching); and session planning (at least one week prior to teaching). Like the teaching approach itself, the planning is an open-ended, continuous process, requiring the teaching team to move back and forth across the three levels. Within each planning level there is a sequence of basic steps which, if followed, will help contribute to a successful experience with the total-environment approach.

Unit Planning

1. Know the stories in the unit well. Spend time together as a team, telling the stories to each other and sharing their significance for each of you. Talk about the feelings of the biblical characters—especially the ones with whom you personally identify.

2. Identify the major subunits of the story you wish to teach to your children. These will be the natural changes of time and/or place within the story. In the unit previously described, the teaching team identified seven subunits.

3. Identify the scenes, or ministages, you will need to set

up in the classroom for each of the subunits. In the subunit "Childhood Days," the room became Nazareth and the teaching team chose four ministages where action would take place: Jesus' home, the marketplace, the synagogue, and a carpenter's shop.

4. Identify the biblical characters of each subunit. Be sure to include both male and female characters, and the common people, as well as the heroes. Jesus, Mary, Martha, and the disciples were stars in the cast, but the Roman soldiers, the merchants in the marketplace, and the crowds who lined the Palm Sunday parade route were important, also.

Subunit Planning

5. Begin to plan for the specific scenes, or ministages, for the first subunit by answering these questions.

   a. Where will you place the scenes in your room?
   b. How can you create the beginnings of a ministage and still leave some scenery making to the children?
   c. What props do you need to gather for each of the ministages?
   d. What activities naturally took place in each of the scenes you have selected? How can you provide materials so the children can experience those same types of activities? (Examples: bread-making in the home; net-making at the seashore; sandwriting by the synagogue; graffiti writing on the jail walls.) You will need a wide variety of activities from which to choose, so brainstorm and make note of all of them. Be prepared to delete from your room any activities the children avoid; to continue those in which they participate; and to add new ones as needed.

6. Decide what roles you, the teachers, will assume in the first session. Gather your costumes and other props you will need.

7. Think about possible emphases for each session of your subunit. Jot these down for future reference.

8. Choose an emphasis that seems most appropriate for the first session of the subunit.

Session Planning

9. Think about your emphasis for the first session of the subunit. What "feeling-into," "meeting-with," "and "responding-out-of" activities could you provide? Some will be formal and distinct; some will be informal and largely improvised, as you and the children interact with each other.

10. "Feel into" your own role as one of the biblical characters. Think about possible types of verbal and nonverbal exchanges you might have with the children in the ministages. You goal here is to help the children make that backward leap from their here-and-now interests in painting, clay, pounding, or weaving into the past world of the biblical story. You goal here also is to "tell" bits and pieces of the story while remaining "in character." It is possible that you will want to play several characters over the course of a session, in order to elicit more varied responses from the children. If so, you will need to think through each of the possible roles you will play.

Continuing Through the Unit

11. Return to step 8 each week to continue planning for the next session.

12. When you are ready to move to the next subunit (remember to start planning two weeks ahead!), return to step 5.

Living the Bible with Children

Summary

Putting the three guidelines together with a learning-center style and a total-environment approach is like using meat and potatoes and vegetables to create a tasty stew. Each of the foods alone is good to eat. But when they are mixed together and slowly cooked with the right seasonings, the result is a delicious new meal. In the same way, one may teach through learning centers, or use the three guidelines in a traditional classroom, or follow a total-environment approach. Each of these alone can be the basis for creative teaching. But when all three interact with each other, seasoned with the teacher's own faith and understanding and love for children, the result can be a powerful way to help children experience the Bible as a Now event. It is a way that creates a readiness for more content-centered learnings in their youth and adult years, when mental abilities are more fully developed. Total-environment teaching of the Bible is like a kindergarten reading-readiness program, in which children are taken on field trips to the fire station, the zoo, and the farm. Both provide for the learners' participation in "real experience," which they will read about later and discuss and interpret abstractly.

9.
Next Steps

So you are an Adventurous Amateur? You have risked and tried some new ideas. Perhaps you were not great, but you have had enough success that you are not satisfied to go back to your former approach to teaching the Bible to children. So what are the next steps for you? Here are some ideas.

1. Attend a class or workshop. Explore your university extension courses or classes in your local adult education programs. You may find resources or persons there to help you develop your skills in creative drama, dance, or storytelling.

2. Watch for church-sponsored workshops. If you do not discover skill workshops from a Christian education perspective, urge your denomination to sponsor some in your region.

3. Build a support group. Be alert for others who are testing new ideas for teaching the Bible. Organize a group of Adventurous Amateurs where you can share and critique one another's lesson plans, and where you can experiment with your own creative new ideas.

4. Create your own filing system. Whenever you "score" a story, place it in your file. Since the way you score it is for your own use, and since the greatest value comes in the doing of it, do not plan to share these.

Develop some planning charts for Bible stories, listing several possible activities for each guideline. These will help you in emergencies!

5. Read, read, read. The following books are listed under each category, in order from the simplest to the most difficult.

Creative Drama

McCaslin, Nellie. *Creative Dramatics in the Classroom,* 2d ed. New York: David McKay Co., 1974. Emphasizes the importance of play in the emotional as well as the intellectual development of children.

Siks, Geraldine Brain. *Creative Dramatics: An Art for Children.* New York: Harper & Brothers, 1960. Widely used as a textbook. Gives illustrations and anecdotes in discussing the characteristics of children of different ages and the materials appropriate for them.

Ward, Winifred. *Playmaking with Children.* New York and London: Appleton-Century Co., 1947. A pioneer work by a distinguished leader in the field of creative dramatics. Includes dramatics in the school, as recreation, and for religious education.

Siks, Geraldine Brain, ed. *Children's Theatre and Creative Dramatics: Principles and Practices.* Seattle: University of Washington Press, 1961. Contains much factual information. Recommended for teachers who wish to become more informed about creative dramatics.

Cheifiz, Dan. *Theatre in My Head.* Boston: Little, Brown, 1971. Of interest to church school leaders. Emphasizes the need to look "into" children, not merely at them. Shares experiences in an experimental workshop on creative drama in an inner-city New York church.

Storytelling

Jordan-Smith, Paul. "Telling Stories: A Conversation with Diane Wolkstein and Paul Jordan-Smith." *Parabola.* Vol. II, No. 4, 1977. Deals with the question, Why tell stories? Includes some favorite stories of these two masters of the art.

Next Steps

McDermitt, Barbara. "Playmaking and Story Dramatization: Bridging the Gap for Very Young Children." *Journal of the Canadian Child and Youth Drama Association.* Winter 1977. Gives a short introduction to the story participation techniques developed by the author.

Williams, Michael E. "Story Theatre: An Interview with Joyce and Byrne Piven." *Explor.* In press. Included in an issue of the journal of Garrett-Evangelical Theological Seminary devoted entirely to story and storytelling. Shares insights into story theater by two performers and teachers who helped pioneer this art form.

Sawyer, Ruth. *The Way of the Storyteller.* New York: Viking Press, 1962. Speaks of storytelling as a folk art and includes both theory of telling and practical applications. Along with Shedlock's book, this volume is used in many storytelling classes. First published in 1942, it grows directly out of Sawyer's long experience as a teller of tales.

Shedlock, Marie. *The Art of the Story-Teller,* 3d ed. New York: Dover Publications, 1951. First published in 1915, this remains one of the best booklength works in the field. Includes a selection of stories for telling and a bibliography updated to 1951.

Crossan, John Dominic. *The Dark Interval: Toward a Theology of Story.* Niles, Ill.: Argus Communications, 1975. Deals specifically with Bible stories. Outlines categories of story and describes how each affects our understanding of the world and society.

Dance

Taylor, Margaret. *Dramatic Dance with Children in Education and Worship.* North Aurora, Ill.: The Sharing Company, 1977. Especially for church school teachers and parents of children five to eleven years of age.

Mettler, Barbara. *Materials of Dance as a Creative Arts Activity.* Mettler Studios, Box 4456, University Station, Tucson, Ariz.

Living the Bible with Children

Price, Ann. *Move When the Spirit Says Move.* Nashville: Graded Press, 1976. Kit with one 12-inch 33 1/3 rpm record, two 14-frame filmslips, a set of 10 cards and leader's guide. For use with middle elementary children. Available from Cokesbury.

Sheehy, Emma D. *Children Discover Music and Dance.* New York: Henry Holt & Co., 1959.

Sonen, Pat. *Using Movement Creatively in Religious Education.* Unitarian-Universalist Association, Department of Education, 25 Beacon St., Boston, Mass., 1963.

Ortegel, Sister Adelaide. *A Dancing People.* The Center for Contemporary Celebration, West Lafayette, Ind., 1976. Describes dance as an authentic expression of faith, available to everyone.

Discussion

Cully, Iris V. *Ways to Teach Children.* Philadelphia: Lutheran Church Press, 1965. Intended for use in leadership development; see especially chapter 6, "Studying and Thinking." Includes leader's guides.

Emswiler, Tom Neufer, and Emswiler, Sharon Neufer. *What Would You Do?* Nashville: Graded Press, 1977. Kit to help middle-elementary children practice decision-making. Includes 30 8-by-10 pictures, a 33 1/3 rpm record, and leader's guide. Available from Cokesbury.

Service Projects

Russell, Letty. *Christian Education in Mission.* Philadelphia: The Westminster Press, 1967.

Sprague, Ruth L., ed. *Building Justice: A Course for Fifth and Sixth Graders.* Philadelphia: United Church Press, 1970.

Total-Environment Way of Teaching

Rood, Wayne. *On Nurturing Christians.* Nashville: Abingdon, 1972. Good basic introduction to presenting Christian education, different from the traditional schooling approach.

Next Steps

See pages 87-89, which describe the total-environment way of teaching, using the example of the Bedouin experience.

Spolin, Viola. *Improvisation for the Theater.* Evanston, Ill.: Northwestern University Press, 1963. Classic textbook for college theater majors that will stretch your mind about what improvisation is and how it is done. Does not deal directly with improvisation in a total-environment way of teaching, but may stimulate you to expand upon the roles you can take in improvising with children in the total-environment approach.

Notes

Chapter One

1. Dorothy Jean Furnish, *Exploring the Bible with Children* (Nashville: Abingdon, 1975), the concept of the Bible as having "unlimited meanings," pp. 40-51.
2. Edward DeBono, *The New Think* (New York: Basic Books, 1968).
3. Jemima Luke, "Sweet Story," 1841, *The Abingdon Hymnal* (New York: Abingdon Press, 1928), p. 266.
4. Wayne Rood, *On Nurturing Christians* (Nashville: Abingdon, 1972), p. 83.

Chapter Two

1. Dorothy Jean Furnish, *Exploring the Bible with Children,* Section I, "The Bible," and Section II, "Children."
2. Mary Lu Walker, *Dandelions* (Paramus, N.J.: Paulist/Newman Press, 1975).
3. *Rejoice and Sing Praise* (Nashville: Abingdon, 1977).
4. *Elementary I-II Student,* Fall 1974, p. 34. Words and music by Pamela Hughes. Copyright © 1973 by Graded Press.

Chapter Four

1. Adapted from a chart designed by Leland H. Roloff, Department of the School of Speech, Northwestern University, for the scoring and analysis of fairy tales, and used in the class "Literature and Body Thinking."
2. Helen Doss, *Young Reader's Book of Bible Stories* (Nashville: Abingdon, 1970).
3. This technique was developed by Barbara McDermitt and has been described in "Playmaking and Story Dramatization: Bridging the Gap for Very Young Children," *Journal of the Canadian Child and Youth Drama Association* (Winter 1977).

Chapter Five

1. Adapted from Margaret Taylor, *Dramatic Dance with Children in Education and Worship,* Doug Adams, ed. (North Aurora, Ill.: The Sharing Company, 1977), p. 10.

Chapter Eight

1. Words and Music by Richard K. Avery and Donald S. Marsh, *Middle Elementary Student,* Winter 1977–78.
2. From "And Jesus Grew," verses 1, 2, and 5 by Ann F. Price. Words and music copyright © 1973 by Graded Press. Verses 3, 4, 6, 7, 8, and 9 were composed by Dorothy Jean Furnish. From *The I-II Teacher,* Winter 1974–75, p. 87. Copyright © 1974 by Graded Press.